HARROW LIBRARY SERVICES

Please return this item by the last date shown. You can renew it by post, phone or in person unless it has been reserved by another library user. Fines will be charged on overdue items if applicable. 392 -5
Thank you for using the library.

The Wedding Survival Guide

Jaclyn C. Hirschhaut
and Kate Taylor

Published in 2004 by
New Holland Publishers (UK) Ltd
London • Cape Town • Sydney • Auckland

Garfield House
86-88 Edgware Road
London W2 2EA
United Kingdom
www.newhollandpublishers.com

10 9 8 7 6 5 4 3 2 1

ISBN 1-84330-681-6

Conceived and produced by
Elwin Street Limtied
35 Charlotte Road
London EC2A 3PD
United Kingdom
www.elwinstreet.com

Editors: Anna Southgate, Jane Morrow
Designer: Thomas Keenes
Illustrator: Robert Shadbolt

Printed in Singapore

Contents

The Proposal 6

Introduction 8

The Engagement 10

Your Wedding Theme 20

Choosing The Venue 34

Planning The Reception 46

What To Wear (And How) 64

The Groom's Guide 82

Three Months To Go 96

Two Months To Go 110

One Month To Go 120

One Week To Go 130

Index 142

The proposal

Dear Diary, I am. . . engaged! Yes, it has finally happened. They said one day my prince would come and he has. John – lovely wonderful John – finally got his knee dirty and asked me to marry him. And I said yes!

Actually, I shouted "Yes". Or, more specifically (and a million times more embarrassing) "Yes please". Ahem.

It all happened last night, on way back from party. I was quite awfully drunk and a little out of control. Had planned to raise the "what are your intentions talk" sometime over the weekend myself. Fed up with dating for 18 months and not knowing what future held. Had planned it all: was going to calmly and rationally ask him if he saw us getting married or setting up home together one day.

That was calm plan. The reality . . .

"Get your hands off me! Not going home with you. Fact, not going anywhere with you. We're going nowhere. It's been over a year and a half now and NO ring. What is your plan, eh, Mister? Stringing me along? Well, you can forget about it."

Everything I had planned to say politely and sensibly came spewing out in a rush. Poor man. What could he do? Well, he COULD have run for his life then and there. He should have, in my view. But no. Displaying an otherwise hidden masochistic streak, he DROPPED TO ONE KNEE. "Kate Taylor, marry me. Will you marry me?"

There, in the rain, one knee, all serious. Looking at me with such an open, honest expression of intent, affection and panic. Thinking he was going to lose me forever unless he offered me what I wanted most: to share his future.

Beautiful moment. Ruined by me suddenly, unpredictably, bursting out laughing. It doubled me over. "What?" he begged, hurt. "What?"

"You don't have to propose, you daft idiot!" I laughed. "I'm only in a mood. I'll get over it. But, if you're offering . . ."

I looked at him. Nowhere in his eyes could I see a shadow of doubt, a shuffle of uncertainty. He was still on his knee and people were starting to watch. So I put him out of his misery. And I said, "Yes please".

Fabulous getting home: kisses and giggles and "Oh my God's". Waking up today: heaven. He didn't want me to think it was a drunken-party thing, so he proposed again, in bed. Almost cried. Both did. So lovely. SO happy.

It's all been mad – cannot believe I'm engaged at all. Know that he is Right Man. Know that I'm doing Right Thing – no doubts at all. Both agreed that want to be married in a year – long engagements are for cowards. Both want kids. Both want cat. All perfect.

Except for one thing: NOW what? ✳

"Congratulations! You're going to be a bride!"

Chances are these words will have quite an effect on you – only it might not be the one that people are most expecting. Instead of feeling uplifted and excited, you are more likely feeling scared and a little bit shaky right now.

The truth is, planning a wedding is wonderful. But it's also frightening, stressful and – no-one will tell you this – capable of inducing neurotic thoughts in even the most calm bride-to-be. Typical panics that arise as the event approaches are that your fiancé might be run over the morning of the wedding; that you'll never manage to look prettier than your chief bridesmaid; and that your father will cause you eternal embarrassment in his speech. Of course, all these fears are unfounded: your fiancé will live to become your husband, your father will be tear-jerkingly sweet and the angels will conspire to give your chief bridesmaid a bad-hair day (for which you will be eternally grateful).

So you should know by now that it is perfectly normal to become a little angsty as you plan the biggest day of your life, and this should prepare you for the fluctuating emotions you will experience over the months to come. You are going to be excited, happy, depressed and frustrated in turns. You will be crazy about your fiancé one morning, only to find yourself mad at him that same afternoon when he refuses to get excited about the flowers.

You'll change your mind about your dress with alarming frequency, and you'll be resentful of anyone who cancels after you spent a month on the seating plan.

In spite of this emotional roller-coaster, however, planning your wedding can be as easy, fulfilling and fun as you always imagined. The key is preparation – and this book. A godsend to brides, *The Wedding Survival Guide* presents the entire wedding process in digestible sections, starting with the engagement right through honeymoon ideas, to the Big Day itself. You will find advice on everything from venues to vows, and will be able to indulge in every bridal fantasy you've ever had.

Do you have to accept the engagement ring he proposes with? How do you go about choosing a wedding theme? Is there a tactful way not to invite his weird Uncle George? And what little touches can be added to make yours a day to remember over anyone else's? It is all here and, with our shared experience, all the resources we've gathered together for your information and your enthusiasm, you simply can't fail to plan the wedding of your dreams – even if your chief bridesmaid simply refuses to have a bad-hair day.

You're going to be a bride! (And you're going to love it.)

Chapter One
The Engagement

Let's get this wedding party started. You're officially engaged. Congratulations! But you know only too well that the questions are already coming. Is it rude to reject his choice of ring if you hate it? Should you announce your engagement in the newspapers? Does anybody have engagement parties these days and, if so, who plays host? Relax. The engagement is the easiest part of the whole affair. It's a time for celebration, not agitation. Here's how to cope with effortless grace.

The engagement

I used to be right-handed: not any more. Since this platinum-and-diamond solitaire (princess cut, naturally) was installed on my ring finger, I'm finding I use my left hand for everything. Hailing a taxi? Up it goes, twinkling in the sunshine. Paying for stuff – my left hand waves the money in front of the salesgirl's like I'm trying to hypnotise her.

 I'm unusually proud of being engaged. I stare at other women's left hands and, if they're not sporting a sparkler like mine, I feel sorry for them. I think they're unloved. (They're probably not – they're doubtless being chased by hordes of attentive millionaires who are just BEGGING to marry them, but they refuse to be chained down to a life of babies and cleaning. . . but I prefer to feel superior.)

Getting the ring was fabulous. J came over to my flat the night before, barely visible behind an armful of champagne and roses, and we spent a giggly evening discussing what kind of ring we'd like. Yes – WE'D like. I was surprised at how firm his views were. I'd always expected it to be completely my choice, that my future husband (whoever he'd be) would be happy for me to wear anything, be it a two-bit bauble or Pepsi ring-pull, so long as I smiled.

It seems not. J said he thought platinum and diamond would be best. I almost argued out of habit, until it sunk in. What? He's insisting I go for platinum and diamond? Oh, OK then. Twist my arm. . . The next day we went to Hatton Garden, hand in hand. After pressing our noses against ten windows we realised that our budget wouldn't stretch to any of the wrist-breaking rocks. Several smaller, more delicate rings – with smaller, more delicate price tags – were affordable though, and I tried on everything until we found THE ring. I just knew. It was square, with chiselled edges, set in a platinum band. It looked exactly like a princess's ring – like a fairytale ring. It made me cry. And that sealed it.

Feel a bit guilty that J has to cough up so much money for me. I know I should think, unquestionably, that "I'm worth it" but, er, I don't. Instead I focus on how happy J seems that he bought me such a beautiful ring. I read somewhere that's how to make men happy – let them do things for you. Seems to work. Hurray!

Not having an engagement party. Is that boring? Have we already settled down to a nothing-happening life? Are we resigning ourselves to never having fun again? Or are we just Not Very Rich? Hmm. We're NVRs — sounds aptly like envious. I am getting v. jealous of brides-to-be who have loads of cash to spend on wedding stuff. But then, I'm not jealous of their partners; nobody is as handsome and funny as J.

Did go to friend's engagement party in a bar last month. That was good — she was out-of-control drunk, and her fiancé ignored her the whole time. Ended up with her crying on the dance floor at 9.30 p.m. Good on you, girl. J says he gives them six months. Seems quite a light sentence — she is very volatile. Wonder if it's the engagement that brings out a woman's psycho tendencies? Ideally, it should boost confidence enough for me to become calm, Dream Woman, who never gets upset and floats through days like total Earth Goddess, secure in the knowledge that I Am Loved. Wish it would. Instead, here I am, trying to write diary with left hand, wondering if I will ever have to see J's Uncle Harry again once we're hitched. Hrrmph.

Not much else. Told ex-boyfriend that I was getting married. Thought I was doing right thing — we'd discussed getting married before (well, he discussed, I sat in mute panic) so thought he should hear it from me. Maybe was wrong — he ended call v. abruptly. Next day I got an e-mail from him saying he'd felt "physically sick" at the news. Calm Earth

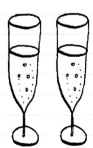

Goddess would not have felt good about that. I did. A tiny, tiny bit. Really tiny, actually, which is still too much. Asked J if he thought that was normal and he said yes, but slightly immature. Sigh. J is so big and grown-up. It'll be good to have a husband around to solve my dilemmas. Like, which colour nail polish goes best with platinum? ✳

The ring

Did he propose and you cried out "yes!"... or did you propose and *he* accept? Whatever the personal circumstances of your engagement, the appearance of a ring on the fourth finger of your left hand will be the first sign that a wedding is in the works.

Traditionally, the groom gets the whole thing going by professing his love, offering a proposal of marriage and presenting a small velvet box containing a dazzling diamond ring. While the height of romance for some of us, this is not the only option and there are a variety of alternatives available to the modern couple. Perhaps your man proposed without a ring, insistent that *you* choose the jewellery you will be wearing daily for the rest of your life; or maybe one of you has a family heirloom ring already. Other ideas are to have fun shopping for antique jewellery together or to seek jewellers who specialise in creating one-of-a-kind designs.

For many couples, the engagement ring will turn out to be the most treasured – and most expensive – wedding item on the list. The responsibility of paying for it rests entirely with your fiancé and, regardless of the amount of money budgeted for it, he should aim for the very best quality he can afford. One rule of thumb is that the price of the engagement ring should equal about two months of the groom's salary.

Buying the ring together

Savvy shoppers will certainly do some homework first. Steer clear of jewellers promoting deep discounts, and take note of word-of-mouth recommendations from friends and family members. Long-standing, well-established jewellery stores are among the most reputable, and are typically staffed by experienced sales personnel who can identify the finest rings within the specified price range.

Choosing the stone

To start with, you should think about your choice of diamonds or coloured gems, and if you want a diamond ring, you should start with the four important characteristics of diamonds: cut, colour, clarity and carat.

The sparkle of your stone is determined by its cut, or the arrangement of a diamond's 58 facets that reflect light. A well-cut diamond sparkles more brilliantly than one of lesser quality.

Colour of a stone can range from clear to hues of blue, pink or yellow. Clear is preferred, since colour is considered to obstruct a stone's capability to reflect light.

Clarity refers to the tiny, natural flaws of a stone that can only be seen under magnification. Diamonds containing the fewest of these inclusions are considered to be of the best clarity and command a higher price.

The weight of a stone is measured in carats and points, with 100 points equalling one carat. Typically, the carat weight is the least important consideration in assessing the value of a diamond.

Birthstones

If you don't want a classic diamond ring, consider instead a birthstone – a tradition said to carry a special meaning in each case:

January – Garnet – Truth
February – Amethyst – Sincerity
March – Aquamarine – Courage
April – Diamond – Purity
May – Emerald – Harmony
June – Pearl – Wisdom
July – Ruby – Love
August – Peridot – Contentment
September – Sapphire – Insight
October – Opal – Good fortune
November – Topaz – Intelligence
December – Turquoise – Success

Popular diamond shapes

The shape is the outer appearance of the stone, while the cut refers to the gem's reflective qualities.

Round – The most popular shape, and the basis for all other shapes.

Oval – A symmetrical shape, which will give an illusion of long hands.

Marquise – An elongated shape with pointed ends.

Pear – Combines the oval and the marquise, and is shaped like a teardrop.

Heart – A pear-shape with a cleft at the top.

Emerald – A rectangle with cut corners.

Princess – A square or rectangle cut with numerous facets.

The design of the ring

Once you have chosen the stone, you can think about the look of the ring. The design should reflect your personal sense of style but should also suit your lifestyle. The metal colour and the shape of the setting should be chosen to enhance the gems. The simplest settings typically show off a beautiful stone best.

If either you or your fiancé has a special stone or perhaps a family ring that has been handed down through generations, a good jeweller will be able to design a new setting to flatter the stone on your finger.

After the wedding, you will most likely wear a separate wedding band. The two aren't required to match, but should coordinate well in fit, design and colour.

It's important to secure a written appraisal of the stone and setting from your jeweller, and to forward a copy to your insurance agent. Precious jewellery should be insured against loss, damage or theft, and your insurance agent can add a rider to your home contents' policy to cover it. It's a good idea to have your rings cleaned and the setting checked by your jeweller every six months.

Announcing the engagement

Now that you've accepted his proposal (or he's accepted yours) you can announce your intentions together... first to your family and then to his. Then, according to proper wedding etiquette, the groom's parents should contact the bride's parents first, to express their delight at the news.

Once your parents have exchanged courtesies, you can start to tell other family members and friends. Telephone and e-mail are acceptable methods for contacting most people today, but handwritten notes should be sent to older, traditionally orientated relatives unless you are able to tell them in person.

Consider whether you want to announce your engagement in a newspaper. If either of you is living away from your hometown, it might be a good idea to place the announcement in more than one local or capital-city newspaper.

Most newspapers provide guidelines for announcing both engagements and weddings, and the parents of the bride usually take responsibility for this (including any fees incurred). Some newspapers allow inclusion of a professional photo of the bride or, more popular today, the engaged couple.

Another option, and one that is growing in popularity, is to announce your engagement over the Internet. It is by far the quickest way of getting news to distant friends and relatives, and has great novelty value as well.

Example of an engagement announcement:

Mr. and Mrs. Anthony Watson
announce the engagement of their daughter
Claire Elizabeth
to
Mr. Thomas Paul Knight, the son of
Mr. and Mrs. Peter Knight of Wimbledon,
London
April 3rd, 2003

If the bride's parents are divorced, their names appear on consecutive lines:

Mr. Anthony Watson
Mrs. George Thomas
announce the engagement of their daughter

Couples hosting their own wedding also make the announcement:

Claire Elizabeth Watson
is to be married to
Thomas Paul Knight
Miss Watson is the daughter of
Mr. Anthony Watson of Ramsgate, Kent
and
Mrs. George Thomas of Farnham, Surrey

Stephen proposed to me in an e-mail, which is typical of him, so it seemed fitting for us to tell everybody about our engagement over the Internet. We found a site that specialised in spreading personal news, wrote a few humorous lines, and then sent an e-mail to everyone we knew, telling them to take a look. It was great to see how quickly people came back to congratulate us. **Sophie, 31**

The engagement party

The real fun starts with a series of parties and gatherings, usually kicked off by your family and closest friends at an engagement party. There are no strict rules here, although here are a few guidelines as to what form celebrations might take.

What are your options?

Most commonly, the first event is hosted by the parents of the groom and can range from a cocktail celebration or dinner party at their home to a casual picnic, afternoon tea or barbecue.

Since the engagement party is usually a much less formal occasion than the wedding celebration, there is the opportunity to invite people you might not be able to include in the wedding guest list, such as extended family, with their young children, neighbours and work friends. Of course, this should be explained to guests tactfully before the party to avoid embarrassment.

If you have settled in a location away from both your hometowns, or if one of you has been married before, you may give your own party to announce the happy news to acquaintances and colleagues. In this case, you might choose to hold an informal gathering and make it clear that gifts are not expected.

Engagement party etiquette

Engagement parties nowadays tend to be open gatherings of family members and friends, rather than smaller affairs that resemble the upcoming wedding. If either the bride or groom has been previously married, these festivities should take a romantic but toned-down ambience.

Depending on the formality of the occasion and the number of guests, invitations to the engagement party can be mailed or telephoned. Food may be a buffet or sit-down meal and a toast is generally made to the prospective newlyweds.

Guests at an engagement party commonly bring gifts of a practical household nature for the couple. You should be prepared for this, and plan to send written thank-you notes within a few days of the party. Also on the subject of thank-you notes, an especially warm one should be sent to the host and hostess of the party, if applicable.

Survival tactics

Whether you were expecting the proposal or not, it does not always follow that you knew how or where your fiancé was going to pop the question. Here are some hints on how to handle a tricky situation, as well as advice on keeping your head in the early days of your engagement.

Accepting a proposal

In most cases your fiancé will have thought long and hard about how to propose, probably asking your friends for advice along the way. If he chooses to get down on one knee in the rain, to pop the question in front of a million friends at a party or to get his best mate to ask you for him, spare a moment for how he must be feeling and the effort he has made. Whatever you do, do

not take too long to say "yes". Every second will seem like a minute to him, and it is cruel to leave him hanging.

Rejecting a ring

What do you do if your fiancé pops the question and presents you with a ring that is not to your taste? The solution lies in a blend of honesty and extreme tactfulness. You are going to have the ring for a long time and it should at least be one you are happy with. Look for something you do like about the ring and suggest changing other aspects to make it more "personal" to you. Timing is crucial here: don't reject the ring the minute, or even the day, he proposes, but you shouldn't leave it longer than a week either.

The "ex" question

One of you is bound to have had a close relationship in the past, perhaps even marriage, where you need to be particularly sensitive in breaking your news. In such cases it is best to call early on in person so that your ex does not hear it from someone else. This is all the more important if either of you has children to consider too.

Keeping your head

Many couples will find themselves caught up in the big moment as they take centre stage for the first time. Be sure to remain sensitive to stressful moments as you try to please everyone involved in your celebration. Learning the art of compromise early is invaluable, as is relying on tried-and-true wedding etiquette to move beyond any sticky situations.

Resources

How to buy a diamond

De Beers
50 Old Bond Street
London, W1S 4QT
Tel: 020 7758 9700
www.debeers.com

Cool Diamonds
100 Hatton Garden
London, EC1N 8NX
Tel: 020 7405 5322
www.cooldiamonds.com

Tiffany & Company
25 Old Bond Street
London, W1S 4QB
Tel: 020 7409 2790
www.tiffany.com

www.weddingchannel.com

www.thediamondbuyingguide.com

www.jewellerywebshop.co.uk

www.adiamondisforever.com

www.diamondgrading.com

Choosing a jeweller

British Jewellery Association
1 Saffron Hill
London, EC1N 8RA
Tel: 020 7404 4444
www.bja.org.uk

www.diamondreview.com

Antique and estate jewellery

Bath Antiques
Bartlett Street Antiques Centre
Bartlett Street
Bath, BA1 2QZ
Tel: 01225 311061
www.BathAntiquesOnline.com

www.bonds-of-london.co.uk

www.antiqueandestate.com

www.faycullen.com

www.jewelrycentral.com

Stationery

Coppins Cards
391 Footscray Road
New Eltham
London, SE9 2DR
Tel: 020 8859 6743
www.coppinscards.co.uk

Marlborough Calligraphy
48 Marlborough Road
Beaston
Derby, DE72 3DD
Tel: 01332 874420
www.marlbcall.com

Chapter Two
Your Wedding Theme

Ever wondered how some brides manage to have the most amazingly coordinated wedding day? It's all in the planning. Once you decide on your theme, you'll find it's suddenly easy to choose the right venue, dress, flowers, readings – everything – to harmonise beautifully. It's just a matter of knowing what you want. Grab a scrapbook and your imagination and start fantasising about your Perfect Day.

My wedding theme

So excited. Today, Anita (bridesmaid) and I sat down to discuss My Wedding Theme. It's going to be so fab! She, like me, thinks I should go for something slightly dramatic and rather "royal". (J says that's just a nice way of calling me a Drama Queen.) Because I'm not your average looking girlie – with this shock of red hair and whiter-shade-of-snow skin – I can get away with unusual styling.

Of course, this is not just about me. The theme should carry through to all areas of the wedding, from flowers to invitations to table dressing to bridesmaids. Even J's buttonhole should, ideally, tone. This calls for major organisation and a fortune's worth of bridal magazines.

LOVE bridal magazines. They're not the height of editorial creativity, but brides-to-be don't want that. What we want is a ton of pictures of brides, flowers and castles, with features telling us how to look stunning for a fiver. After a day's reading, have made following decisions:

Theme: Bride of Dracula
Description: dramatic dress, castle (or similar), J in tails, blood-red roses, candelabras. . .
Where: somewhere in Kent (near my parents)
Bridesmaids: Anita and Becky (J's niece)
My hair: up, with twiddly tendrils
Invitations: equally dramatic – handmade paper, copperplate writing, black card
Wedding car: London taxi

Yes, I know the London taxi doesn't really go with the theme, but they're my favourite cars and I always wanted one. Ideally (a word I find I use eight times a day lately), the reception would be held outdoors, with a table properly laid-up – snowy-white tablecloths billowing, candelabras dripping – on the lawns. Like an outdoor dinner party. It'd be so dramatic and fabulous. So original and different. So memorable and. . .

"Cold" said Mum. "And maybe wet and definitely hard to arrange. Why on earth can't you go for something practical?"

ARGH! It's my wedding. MY special day. Why can't she just be pleased and supportive? Tried to fume for hours after that phone call but found I couldn't, as slightly agreed with her point. It would be a shame if it rained – it'd be ruined. And maybe burning candles and billowing tablecloths weren't ideal tablemates.

Decided to tone it down. To keep the "dramatic" theme, maybe J and I could marry in a country hotel? With lovely grounds and big dining hall. I could wear long gorgeous dress, he could be in tails, and we could have ivy and roses twining everywhere. Anyway, am seeing J tomorrow so will discuss. So good to have a man to share these decisions.

Bloody men! Interfering b*&%$*s! All I got from J was a stunned silence then hysterical laughter. He thought it was stupidest thing he'd ever heard. Has he NO imagination? OK, maybe the Dracula bit is a little nuts, but you have to start mad and tone it down. Otherwise it just gets boring.

He has always wanted a small, quiet wedding in the country. Who knew? Who would have thought men plan things like that? He pictured me in a simple white dress, looking like an English rose (?!), and a reception looking over rolling hills. He wants simple and small, I want dramatic and memorable. He says "tomato" and I say "ugh, salad". He likes minimalism, I like OTT. Lets call the whole thing off. . .

It's going to have to be a compromise, and that worries me. Do not want to "settle" on wedding day. Too important. Marriage is something you only do, ooh, four times in your life, so want to do it right.

But, actually. . . after a chat, there are things that J and I agree on. Like the country thing. That was in my vision too, so we can work on that. And he does want to wear something slightly Mr Darcy-esque. It's going to HAVE to be simple and small because our budget is, well, bijou. And maybe the castle is a bit too Madge and Guy Ritchie. Need to think. But this proves that the engagement stage is important – learning to accommodate each other's dreams and wishes to get something we both want.

But I'll miss Dracula. That would've been so cool. ✳

Where to start

It is perfectly normal to have mixed feelings about planning your wedding, especially as there seems to be so much that needs doing right from day one. The best place to start is by talking about the style of wedding you both would like and taking notes of all of your ideas.

First, think about what's most important to the two of you and make lists of the various elements that would make the day perfect, from the obvious through to your wildest dreams; remember, this is a chance to express your personal style. Pinpoint areas you won't budge on as well as aspects where you can be flexible. Begin a realistic conversation about financing the wedding and where the money to cover the expenses will come from. Set up a time to speak with each of your families to determine how they can contribute to the budget.

As you begin to firm up your decisions, it will soon become apparent that you may have to make some compromises along the way; one decision often impacts another and you will need to adapt accordingly. It is important for you to be prepared to make adjustments while still keeping your priorities in focus.

When to get married

Similar to planning any other type of special event, the simplest plans require the shortest time in arranging, while more elaborate celebrations with fine-tuned details will demand more time and more money.

Organising a wedding celebration typically spans at least six months to a year or more. At the beginning, it may seem like an inordinate amount of time is spent in making preparations for an event that primarily lasts just one day. But, with the help of your fiancé, your families, your closest friends and a flurry of professionals, you will soon get into it. Be realistic about the amount of time you'll need for shopping

and setting up the arrangements, and build in a little cushion of an extra week or so. If your time is short or you have extra money, consider hiring a professional wedding consultant to guide you through the process (see page 30).

Weddings take place during every month of the year, and you'll want to consider a time when the weather will be ideal and guests can travel to the location easily.

Selecting the day itself is sometimes the result of coordinating your families' schedules with the availability of the professionals you want to hire. All facilities and party professionals are in higher demand during certain times of the year – notably the spring and summer months – and are busier on certain days over others, namely Saturdays. Having a little flexibility within your desired timeframe might allow money savings and assure that fulfilling your dream is less complicated.

Furthermore, the last thing that you would want to experience is that you're so exhausted from planning all the details that you can't be rested, relaxed and ready to thoroughly enjoy the time surrounding your wedding day. So avoid scheduling your wedding at a time that's expected to be busy for you or your fiancé, and away from other family commitments or major projects at work.

Choosing a theme

Most brides-to-be will have fantasised about their wedding day at some time or other. Think back to when you were a little girl and you probably remember playing "dress-up" to a fairytale wedding story yourself, wearing a sparkling evening dress and a princess tiara and your handsome fiancé riding onto the scene on the most magnificent horse.

Fast-forward to today, and your image of you and your fiancé may well have a different look to it. This does not mean there cannot be a sense of enchantment surrounding your wedding celebrations, however. Big or small, country or city, every wedding takes on a wedding style that is tied to the bride and groom and their own dreams of how their day should be.

More often than not, a theme will evolve from the season in which you wed; think about the stunning flowers that can inspire a spring- or summertime wedding, while the vivid foliage of autumn is ideal for the cooler months. And what better inspiration for an all-white theme than a perfect winter wonderland setting. Other sources for inspiration might include bygone eras, classic fairytales, the honeymoon destination (although your fiancé might prefer to keep this a surprise) and the location of the ceremony and reception.

Making it unique

When it comes to saying your vows, the surroundings you choose can be as familiar as your own home, your neighbourhood church or synagogue, a nearby landmark or an exotic destination.

Similarly, the invitations, decorations, music, food and drink can be chosen to complement the basic theme of your wedding and reflect your personal style as a couple. Remember, too, that the congregation of guests who witness your wedding is an especially vital ingredient, and that many of the special touches will be chosen primarily with them in mind.

Following are some ideas on how to use a central theme and tie in various aspects of your wedding:

* In a garden or casual setting, consider a country-style wedding with invitations printed on handmade paper with pressed flowers. Arrange the bridesmaids' bouquets in baskets and base the reception on a simple buffet of your favourite summer foods. Drape the dining tables in floral or chequered cloths decked with eyelet-trimmed napkins, and place a miniature vase of cut flowers at each setting. Offer seed packets to guests as they leave the reception, where folk music and traditional dancing is part of the entertainment.

* In a tropical setting, decorate with vivid, citrus colours of orange, yellow and lime. Fill the venue with native flowers, trees and palm fronds. Choose a menu of grilled foods and decorate the plates with edible petals. Serve fruity drinks inspired by the local habitat and seal the ambience with music from a steel drum band.

* For a super-cool, cold-weather wedding, create a winter wonderland by filling the setting with numerous ivory candles in hurricane sleeves and votives. Decorate small trees in tiny twinkling lights to frame the site or set dry ice in water to create a cloud-like stage. Pass cups of steaming, hot mulled cider or wine as guests arrive at the reception.

* Focus on your favourite colour for a design theme, introduced first in the envelope sleeve of your wedding invitation. Choose a complementary tone for the bridesmaids' gowns and the mothers' corsages. Fill your ceremony and reception venues with flowers, balloons or candles in coordinated coloured tones. Dress the reception chairs in fabric loose covers, and trim favours for the guests with matching ribbon.

* Opt for an old-time, Victorian theme where flowers, vintage lace and formality reign supreme. Choose a delicate script for the typeface on the wedding invitations and hire a calligrapher to address the envelopes. Order silver holders for the bridesmaids' bouquets. Dress the ushers in formalwear complete with top hats, gloves, spats and walking sticks. Use antique glass vases, old-fashioned teapots or silver urns to hold centrepieces and decorate each place setting with embellished miniature frames that serve as the guest favour.

* Schedule your wedding near a holiday, especially Christmas or Valentine's Day and you'll have an automatic theme to work around.

I thought Michael was joking when he said he wanted to get married in Hawaii. It sounded so out of our reach. But he persevered and we found a company that took care of all the arrangements from the flights out there, to the celebrant, to the fruit cocktails at the reception. All the bridesmaids wore grass skirts and the ushers leis. Cheesy, maybe, but I would do it again tomorrow. **Julia, 27**

The guest list

For some brides, a wedding just wouldn't be a wedding without a large crowd of friends and relatives. For others, a purposefully small wedding party is preferred. The choice is influenced by the budget as well as the capacity of the ceremony and reception venues.

The wedding party

The wedding party will comprise favourite family members and friends who surround the two of you on the day, contributing one way or another to the unfolding events.

✳ The chief bridesmaid is, traditionally, the bride's closest unmarried friend, often her sister, and the matron-of-honour is her closest married friend or relative. She is the last bridesmaid to walk down the aisle behind other bridesmaids and the bride, and during the ceremony she holds the bride's bouquet, and arranges the bride's veil and train as necessary.

✳ The bridesmaids can be the sisters, cousins and friends of the bride who support her during the engagement and bring her to marriage. They follow her as she processes up the aisle on the arm of her father.

✳ The father of the bride traditionally "gives" her in marriage, although the duty can also be handled by a stepfather, brother, uncle or close family friend.

✳ The mother of the bride is distinguished as the last guest to be seated for the ceremony and is considered the official hostess of the wedding reception.

✳ The best man is the groom's best friend or relative who stands up front with him as the marriage ceremony begins, and who is responsible for delivering the rings at the ceremony and acting as an usher, if necessary. Many grooms ask their brother to serve as their best man.

✳ The ushers support the groom during the engagement and bring him to marriage.

✳ Many weddings have a scattering of young children – usually just those of siblings and close friends – some of whom are also given tasks to perform: a page boy carries an ornate pillow on which symbolic wedding rings are tied, while the flower girl follows and scatters flower petals in the bride's path.

Choosing your bridesmaids

Your most likely choice for bridesmaids will be your sisters and/or your best friends that you have formed since primary school through to present day. There may also be chosen from members of your fiancé's family that you would wish to take on the role.

The invitation to be a bridesmaid is one a girl either relishes or dreads. For some it is a dream come true and there is not enough they can do to support a true friend. For others the fear of having to wear some monstrous outfit overrides the pleasure of being selected. Try to anticipate the reactions of your chosen few and be prepared to dispel/instill enthusiasm accordingly.

Since being a bridesmaid requires a substantial financial commitment to cover the cost of an outfit, travel expenses, participating and planning your hen night, and choosing a wedding gift, you should give each one time to be sure she's comfortable with her role from the beginning. If not, give her the opportunity to take another special role at the wedding, such as presenting a reading or a prayer during the service. Also, don't feel obliged to ask a friend or relative just because you were a bridesmaid at their wedding.

One of the big challenges will be keeping everyone informed of the details as the wedding celebration falls into place. Let them know about any pre-wedding parties so that they can make plans to be there, as well as have an idea about the kind of party so that they're properly dressed for the occasion. Give them information on the rehearsal as soon as possible, and keep your unmarried bridesmaids up to date on single groomsmen at the wedding.

If the expense of being in your wedding is mounting, you might try to ease the burden by assisting with accommodation during the wedding period. If everyone can't stay at your own home, maybe a few of your neighbours would be willing to offer up their guest rooms so that everyone can be close to the centre of activity. Or check out the rate at some nearby hotels and group the bridesmaids together in pairs or groups.

One final point is to try to have the same number of maids as ushers. This way you avoid any embarrassment with the seating at the reception or following your first dance when the music starts.

Make it special
Given that each of your bridesmaids might be stressed before (and on) the big day, think of ways to make them feel at ease and reward them for their spirited devotion to your cause!

✳ Book appointments for manicures and pedicures together.

✳ Treat them to a special bridesmaid's luncheon or brunch on the day before the wedding.

✳ Present each one with a sentimental gift, along with a genuine note of how important her friendship and help has been during your engagement.

✳ Make time to speak personally with each bridesmaid on your wedding day.

✳ Send a postcard to each attendant while you are on honeymoon.

✳ Once you return, make plans to reconnect for a girls' night out together.

Do you need a wedding planner?

So many details… so little time! Exactly how much time do you have to plan your marriage ceremony and the reception that will follow? For a growing number of brides, the help of a professional wedding planner is a surprisingly cost-effective service that can take your ideas and turn them into reality.

Even the simplest wedding celebration requires countless hours of careful planning and dedicated attention to a vast number of details. Not only will you need help in choosing the right wedding specialists for the day, but you'll also want to avoid making potentially embarrassing mistakes. A consultant can become your best friend as you work together to take the effort out of creating the perfect wedding.

There are times when the services of a professional consultant are especially helpful to the bride and groom; for example, if you are planning a long-distance wedding or you need neutral advice where your or your fiancé's parents are divorced and there are extra opinions and needs to satisfy under pressure. Similarly, when keeping to budget is a high priority, a professional wedding planner can advise on spending wisely and steering clear of costly mistakes. He or she can help to negotiate the contracts with the service providers, making sure that no detail is forgotten.

And, of course, a wedding planner is the obvious option if you are reluctant to handle the inevitable mountain of telephone calls and appointments yourself and want to avoid facing difficult questions and challenging dilemmas. You will also be able to relax completely on your wedding day, confident that any last-minute crisis will be expertly handled by someone else!

Hiring a wedding planner

While some brides hire consultants to handle the entire event, others sign them on to take over specific assignments. Obviously, the decision is usually dependent upon the budget. Professional wedding planners can be paid by the hour or they can charge an agreed-upon percentage of the fees from the caterer, florist and musicians that they book on your behalf. The relationship between the bride and the consultant should be settled at the first meeting, and before any planning begins.

Finding a wedding planner

The preferable option is by word of mouth. If you have a friend or relative who raves about the service they got, snap up the phone number. Otherwise look out for features and listings in bridal magazines.

When best to hire help?

Decide what is best for your particular situation and budget when hiring consultants

- To give general party planning advice and local suppliers at an early stage.

- To take care of specific aspects that aren't familiar to you or your families.

- To direct a rehearsal and make sure everything runs smoothly on the Big Day.

- To handle every detail and be on hand until you leave for the honeymoon. Budget for 10–15 per cent of the total bill.

The budget

If you haven't done so already, now is the time to sit down and set a realistic budget. The cost of a wedding is dependent upon one factor: time. The more time you have to shop around for the best deal, the more money you might save.

On the other hand, if you want to be married sooner rather than later, you'll most likely grab details of the wedding that appeal to you as soon as you find them, regardless of the price tag. By drawing up a budget, you will accomplish two objectives. First, it will help to provide a realistic plan for how much money you will need altogether. Secondly, by listing all the different elements separately, you will provide yourself with a checklist of details which can then be ordered and arranged in terms of priority and/or cost.

Start by compiling two lists: essentials and desirables. The secret is to juggle some to accommodate others until you have a good balance of both. Phone around or look on the Internet to get an initial idea of likely costs, bearing in mind that, as a rule, the more formal the wedding, the more expensive it will be. There is always the possibility that you will go over budget on some areas of planning, and you should have a contingency plan for dealing with this. (See Tips for saving money, page 32).

How the budget breaks

- 40 per cent for the reception food and beverages.
- 12 per cent for the bride's clothes.
- 12 per cent for the ceremony and reception music.
- 11 per cent for miscellaneous expenses.
- 10 per cent for the bouquets and decoration flowers.
- 10 per cent for photography.
- 5 per cent for invitations and stationery.

There will also be miscellaneous expenses to consider, such as the site usage cost for the ceremony plus fees for the celebrant and wedding director, the wedding rings, transportation for the wedding party, the attendants' gifts, the bride's honeymoon trousseau and the cleaning and preservation of the bridal gown.

Survival tactics

Make the right choices now and you will avoid countless unnecessary complications or upsets as your plans develop. The two key areas are communication and budget; you and your fiancé should know the direction you are going in from the start, and understand the need to keep a close eye on your finances.

Don't forget your fiancé!

It's all too easy for a bride to get wrapped up in her own grand plan, almost completely forgetting to consider her fiancé's vision of the Big Day. This is made easier still by the groom's seeming lack of interest in the finer details. Don't take this as a bad omen – he just hasn't been planning this since he was six years old – and don't cut him out of the process altogether. There really are aspects that he will (and should) want to have input in, so be sensitive to including him in making those decisions.

Keep it real

Make sure you choose something you are both happy with. There is no point arranging a beach party if the idea of hot sun and sand is bottom of your list for comfort; if you prefer casual get-togethers with friends and family, top hat and tails may not be for you. On the other hand, if you love the idea of a cocktail party, make this your starting point and expand the theme from there.

Don't overdo it

While there is no doubt that it is the sum of all the details that will eventually create the day of your dreams, there's a real danger of going way overboard in your eagerness to create the "perfect" wedding.

Keep the various aspects of your theme simple and make sure there are no hideous clashes. Rather than trying to have a little of everything, concentrate on linking the ceremony and celebrations with a few key elements for maximum style.

Tips for saving money

By making some smart decisions on the front end, you will be able to make some money-saving choices that do not compromise your original dreams for your wedding day.

* The most obvious consideration is the size of the guest list. For couples with limited funds, think about hosting a small wedding with just your immediate family and closest friends, and having a special party for your larger circle of friends at a later date.

* The scheduling of your wedding can also have a direct effect on costs if you select off-peak times. You could choose to be married on a Thursday night or a Sunday afternoon to avoid the premiums placed on Saturday affairs. Alternatively, opt for a daytime celebration rather than an evening one and take advantage of serving a brunch or lighter meal at the reception.

* Rather than reaching out to professionals to produce all the elements of your wedding, you can take on some of the parts yourself with the assistance of family and friends. Enlist the help of your sisters, cousins and bridesmaids to help out with the simple but laborious tasks.

* One word of caution, however, is to not take chances on the quality of what you can do yourself, especially for the parts of the wedding that are most important to you.

Resources

Theme weddings

Fantaysia
The Homestead,
Thurnscoe Road,
Bolton-on-Dearne,
Rotherham, S63 8JW
Tel: 01709 894090
www.fantaysia.co.uk

All About Weddings
66 Montpelier Road
Brighton, BN1 3BL
Tel: 01273 723459

All For You Weddings
5 The Moorlands
Benson, OX10 6RT
Tel: 07904 251847

Wedding Wonders
18 Gidea Close
Gidea Park
Romford, RM2 5NP
Tel: 01708 743240

www.day2remember.com

www.todays-weddings.com

Destination weddings

Honeymoon Heaven
34 Manchester Road
Southport, PR9 9AZ
Tel: 01704 530415
www.honeymoonheaven.co.uk

Barefoot Luxury
204 King Street
London, W6 0RA
Tel: 020 8741 4319
www.BarefootLuxury.com

Exclusive Weddings in Scotland
The Old Schoolhouse
Forteviot, PH2 9BT
Tel: 01764 684529

The Wedding Club
142 Old Station Road
Hampton-In-Arden
Solihull, B92 0HF
Tel: 07976 848793

Weddings and Honeymoons Abroad (MK)
11 Darby Close
Shenley Lodge, MK5 7EX
Tel: 01908 690201

Viva Las Vegas
1205 Las Vegas Blvd
South Las Vegas
Nevada 89104, USA
Tel: (800) 574 4450
www.vivalasvegasweddings.com

Vacations To Go
1502 Augusta Drive, Ste 415
Houston, TX 77057, USA
Tel: (800) 338 4962
www.resortvacationstogo.com

www.disney.go.com

www.weddings-abroad.com

Wedding showstoppers

Fireworks Connections
No. 4, 90 Warrior Square
St Leonards on Sea, TN37 6BP
Tel: 01424 438497

Flashpoint Fireworks Limited
19 The Meadows
Chester Road
Aldershot, GU12 6BB
Tel: 01252 641014

Ice Creations
Unit 7K
Lodge Rd
Staplehurst, TN12 0QY
Tel: 01580 892977
www.icecreations.tv

Chapter Three
Choosing The Venue

Choosing where to get married may be the main decision you'll have to make. Not only do you have to decide whether to have a religious or civil ceremony, but wherever you host the reception has to be accommodating, available, *affordable*, and needs to fit in with your wedding theme (your fiancé has to like it too). These days you are allowed to get married almost anywhere, from castle to cabin cruiser. You could hire a cinema and be the main feature. Your groom could say his vows from the bow of a ship. You could fly to Antigua, Italy, Morocco. . .

Choosing the venue

I am *so* tired – fell asleep on the train this morning. Up all night celebrating my betrothal in all manner of exotic, double-jointed ways. If only. In fact, sex has left the building. J and I haven't so much as brushed past each other for the last – Oh My God – five days. I think it's because we've been seeing so much of my parents.

Fab weekend. J took us to five different venues to check out wedding facilities. We agreed on which we liked best too, which was a blessing. It is gorgeous – attached to a vineyard, with stunning grounds, and we get to hold the reception in a huge old stable. They've got rooms for people to stay in, too, which is handy for some of our longer-distance guests. Not sure if we'll stay there, though – J says he hasn't thought that far yet!

So we've booked it provisionally – have even named a date. Gulp. Having a fixed date really brings it all home. But will be good to have final date to tell people. Whenever have to say, "No, we haven't finalised the date yet", I always feel that what they hear is, "No, I can't pin him down to commitment at all. He clearly doesn't love me".

Arranged second viewing of venue with Mum and Dad for next weekend. Mum excited, Dad a bit too. Me? Guilty for taking up all of J's weekends with wedding stuff. (Stupid, as is his wedding too.) Think I need early night. Am getting v. paranoid.

It's booked! And properly. Dad has paid a deposit. So excited. Looked even better this time round, and J looked v. proud of self for finding it. Mum got misty-eyed as we looked at the huge old-beamed stable where the ceremony will take place. There are huge gardens rolling down to river. Swank-central. And a massive bar. Bliss, because I think I'll need a gallon of G&T on Big Day.

The hotel gave us loads of stuff to take home, so I now have proper Wedding File started. Feel organised at last. Plus can finally start thinking about dress design too, now know setting of wedding. The vineyard is quite old, so could go for big, dramatic number. Wish I'd gone for winter wedding now, so could have worn velvet and fake fur. But then I'd have been getting married in less than 6 months... so maybe I don't...

Of course, even though venue has been chosen, no reason to stop viewings altogether. They are v. fun way of getting to snoop round posh hotels and get coffee and cookies free. So Jules (ex-flatmate) and I called up some more hotels and arranged "viewings". Was her idea. I had no part in it. . . Except I was the official bride and had to do most talking. It was fun but scary as she had booked us into most posh hotels she could think of.

At one I think we were busted immediately. Jules asked to see the honeymoon suite and ran riot in it, opening mini bar and getting in bath. So embarrassing. I had to distract man showing us round, by asking grown-up questions about parking facilities and availability, all while Jules is hopping round behind man, mouthing, "I have stolen the champagne – it's in my handbag". Crippling. Man started to get sniffy when I got giggles, so Jules announced airily that somewhere else had better tea and coffee making facilities and dragged me out. Doubled over with giggles. Am sure will be put on hotel's "most wanted" list of people never to accept bookings from.

Told J about it later as was sure he'd think it was funny. Was surprised: he was on a downer. Asked him why. OK, bugged him until he caved in and told me why, and he was having worries that he'd never be able to keep me in posh style. Said that when he saw me in all those hotels he realised that I loved them, but that he'd never be able to take me away to posh places like that. He was upset.

Me too. Can't he see that it's him I want, not a lifestyle? No amount of free Aveda showercaps and mini bars could replace what I've found in him: laughter, love and lust. All in one person. Tried to explain that but all came out wrong, so showed him instead. ✳

The art of compromise

Once caught up in the flurry of planning a wedding celebration, it is quite easy to lose sight of the fact that the single most important event of the day is the ceremony itself. Long after the last flower petal is tossed, the bottom line is that you will have become legally, physically and emotionally bound to your husband.

Whether you choose to be married in a house of worship or prefer a civil option on neutral ground, your ceremony should be spiritual – a reflection of your love and dedication to each other. This spirituality can be captured as much by the traditions of your own faith as it can by the roles of family members and friends who contribute on the day. So give thought to what will be said and who will be saying it.

For brides who share the same faith as their husbands-to-be, there is a tendency to follow a set pattern, usually established by the religion in question. This does not have to be the case, however, and even the most traditional marriage ceremony calls for something more personal when it comes to exchanging vows and rings, the readings, music and decorations.

If, as with many couples, your marriage is to be a combination of faiths that includes two officiants and a blend of religious rites, take care not to get too caught up in the preferences of your respective cultures and families, as you will find yourselves having to make compromises in order to satisfy everyone.

Parents are often interested in preserving traditions, especially in the union of couples from different ethnic or religious backgrounds. Despite the fact that marriages of mixed faiths are no longer uncommon, couples still tend to endure mixed reactions from their family members and friends.

The savvy bride will become a conciliator, making every effort to include her future in-laws in the wedding plans, listening to their thoughts, no matter how unrealistic they may seem, and trying to respond to their ideas with simple adaptations to her plans.

The best of both worlds

When planning an interfaith wedding, be careful to incorporate customs and traditions from both sides wherever possible. This will help each family feel included and should avoid any impression of being shut out.

Religious laws sometimes prevent clergy from performing interfaith marriages, although there are often certain members who will agree to counsel and marry couples of differing beliefs in a uniquely customised ritual.

" Jeff was raised in a small Pentecostal community and my parents are quite staunch Catholics, so we knew that our marriage would need to be discussed with sensitivity on both sides. After much discussion our respective officiants agreed to a ceremony that blended different aspects of our two faiths. I believe it was a truly uplifting experience for all of us. " **Juliette, 37**

Your choice of ceremony

Once the two of you have decided whether you want a religious or secular service, it's time to determine where and when the ceremony will take place, and who will be officiating for you.

While there is something undoubtedly special about an outdoor wedding ceremony, the right weather cannot be guaranteed, and so more couples opt for the ultimate control of an indoor ceremony site.

Almost all houses of worship and many hotels, historic homes and such are geared up to serving as the backdrop for a wedding. For something more intimate, or with a limited guest list, why not think about using your parents' home or a faraway destination?

Religious ceremonies

Only you can choose whether to be married in a chapel, church or synagogue – yours, his, the one that either of you belonged to when growing up, or a completely neutral site. Since the marriage ceremony is the main event of the wedding celebration, you'll want to book the site as soon as possible. (In cases where the house of worship does not charge a fee, you should plan to make a donation in honour of your clergyman or rabbi.)

Ask your clergyman or rabbi to help you schedule the wedding to avoid religious holidays. Consider the month, the day of the week and the time of day in terms of tradition, ease of travelling to the desired location and your budget. Just like planning any other special event, you may find significant financial savings by choosing off-peak dates and times. In some major metropolitan cities, hosting a wedding on a weeknight is considered *de rigeur* and is measurably less expensive.

Ideally, the officiant will be someone that has a personal relationship to you or your groom. He or she may be your family clergyman or, perhaps, even an ordained family member. In the event that your celebrant has been recommended to you by someone else, you should verify his or her credentials to be sure that they are properly licensed and are authorised by the religious organisation.

Every house of worship has its own requirements and procedures for being married, which may well include a requirement for pre-marriage counselling (see page 104). Find out exactly what this involves in order to allow enough time to complete the classes and resolve any issues that may arise.

Couples of different faiths may choose to invite each of their respected officiants to perform the ceremony together, or they may conduct two separate services.

Second marriages

Special considerations may be necessary if either one of you has been previously married. You must be sure to comply with the precepts of the faith as dictated by the clergyman. Some denominations do not consent to the conduct of a second wedding, while others may mandate special premarital counselling.

The ceremony at a second wedding is typically simple, with family members and close friends in attendance. Usually, the wedding party consists of just one attendant each and may include children of the couple. Depending on the layout of the location, the couple and their attendants take their place at the foot of the altar without the additional processional or giving away of the bride.

Civil ceremonies

A civil ceremony is probably the right choice for you if resolving differences of faith proves too great, or if neither one of you is especially religious. While the essence of the union will be secular, some celebrants may allow you to integrate the odd traditional wedding rite into the service.

The most straightforward civil ceremony involves heading to a registry office and saying "I do" in front of a celebrant and witnesses. But, just for a moment, imagine yourself stepping down the grand staircase of a turn-of-the-century mansion or exchanging vows in a picturesque garden, or on the porch of a charming country inn. Or say you have always dreamed of getting wed on a sun-drenched beach or halfway up a mountain; anything is possible.

Choosing an unusual location, other than a house of worship for your marriage ceremony, can supply the perfect ambience for your once-in-a-lifetime wedding celebration, whether the place is stately and elegant or relaxed and casual. The real beauty of this type of wedding is that it enables you to arrange both the ceremony and reception in adjacent venues, cutting down on transportation and maximising the time actually spent partying.

Consider the vast number of alternative locations to choose from, including hotels, resorts, public gardens and parks, but also museums, theatres and landmark buildings. Many of these kinds of locations will have their own coordinator for such an occasion – somebody to work with in organising the day's events. Although you will ultimately be responsible for any arrangements made, the coordinator can help you by divulging the details of previous successful weddings at the site and by pointing out any restrictions or limitations of the venue. He or she might even have a photograph album of weddings for ideas, and references from other couples who have used the venue for weddings in the past.

Be sure to ask about the legal requirements of being married at the venue.

As with every major aspect of your wedding, you'll want to enter into a contract with the venue, outlining the services that will be provided to you as well as your responsibilities. Usually, a 50 per cent deposit is paid at the signing of such a contract, with the balance due on the wedding day.

Couples travelling overseas will need to verify the necessary documentation (birth certificates, passports, visas, inoculations, proof of divorce) and check residency requirements for being married abroad with the embassy or tourism bureau (see page 43). Double-check the requirements for religious and civil ceremonies and determine how much time is necessary to complete any paperwork.

" Tom and I wanted our wedding day to be special but not religious or municipal. When the registrar told us we could marry in a beautiful old Chelsea bar we jumped at the chance. We felt really relaxed in this environment and my uncle reckoned it was the best wedding he'd ever been to – although we did have to carry him home later! " **Kate, 40**

Words and music

Once you have decided on either a religious or civil ceremony, the next step is to find the words and music that best suit the occasion while reflecting the personalities of both you and your fiancé.

Religious ceremonies may be marked with special verses of scripture, poetry readings, communion service or the lighting of a unity candle. For a civil ceremony you can opt for poetry and readings too, but not of a religious nature. In both instances, your celebrant will be able to offer direction.

One of the most significant parts of your marriage ceremony is the exchanging of vows. If you are religious you may decide to follow the classic wording from your faith's prayer book. But this is also a chance to create vows of your own. You can draw inspiration from the qualities you admire in each other, poetry, sonnets, song lyrics, passages from books or movies, or your own ethnic heritages.

The music you choose will be a key component of your wedding theme. Some of your selections will have a significance for you as a couple while others should mark specific events during the day.

What are your options?

Churches, chapels and synagogues tend to have limits on the type of music that can be played. You can ask your church leader for guidelines, but you should also consult the church, chapel or synagogue wedding/music director. It's also important to consider early on if additional musicians or vocalists are permitted to participate in the service. Meet with the church organist to determine the breadth of his or her musical range as well as their willingness to perform a piece of music you select or be joined by additional musicians.

The basic categories of ceremony music include the prelude, tunes played as guests are seated; the processional, the beginning of the marriage service; and the recessional at the conclusion of the service. The prelude music sets the stage for the ceremony and should help to create the personal mood for the entire wedding celebration. Choices for the processional and recessional are often exchangeable; most often couples make a stately selection for the processional and a purely joyful selection for the recessional.

Take time to consider incorporating any special songs into the ceremony from a range of liturgical, classical or secular selections. Asking a friend or family member with exceptional musical talent to take part will bring an added personal significance to the occasion.

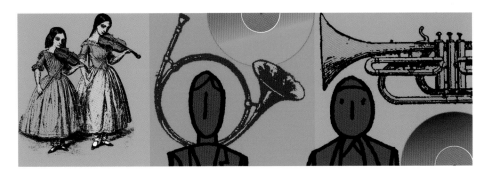

A wedding in paradise

Have you ever dreamed of being married in a tropical setting, surrounded by your loved ones, where your wedding and honeymoon can be rolled into one glorious adventure? Opting for a destination wedding might be the answer for one-stop shopping and some of the simplest wedding planning around.

Destination weddings are not limited to tropical locations; country inns, lakeside resorts and mountain lodges are equally charming settings. The best hotels and inns have wedding consultants on site to take care of arranging everything. They will organise food, hire musicians and a photographer and specify the decorations and bouquets. You can have help picking out the perfect spot for the ceremony outside, with provisions made for an unexpected downpour. You can choose between an impressive garden, a picturesque lake, a breathtaking waterfall or a quiet point along the ocean shore.

Most brides bring their own wedding dress, and the groom can often rent his attire on location. You may wish to incorporate some of the local flavour in your accessories. Your budget can dictate how elaborate the celebration will be, from the most detailed to something as simple as cake and champagne after the ceremony.

What do you need to know?

Choosing a foreign location will add a unique and significant flavour to your wedding celebration, but you need to be sure that all local requirements are met. Check with the authorities in your own country as to whether they too have legal requirements in terms of this.

The tourist bureau of the destination country is the primary source of necessary documentation. In addition to a passport, some locations require a visa and specific inoculations. The most important detail in planning a wedding abroad is to allow enough time, typically a minimum of six to eight weeks, for the processing of all necessary paperwork.

Passport applications can be filed, usually by appointment and interview, at your local post office. For each application you must provide proof of citizenship, two passport photographs, a completed application form and your fee payment. A visa is obtained by sending an application to the consulate of the destination country, along with both of your passports.

The marriage certificate

Unless you are marrying in the Church of England by Banns or Common Licence, notice of the marriage must be given to your Registry Office. Both of you must have resided in the registration district for at least seven days before giving notice, after which you must wait a further 16 days before the marriage can take place. A notice of marriage is valid for 12 months.

There are nationally set fees for giving notice and for the registrar's attendance on the day of the marriage.

England and Wales follow the same legal procedures and stipulations. The General Registry in Scotland and Northern Ireland require that notice be given up to three months prior to, and no later than 15 days before the date of marriage. It is necessary to contact the registrar to have a Marriage Schedule prepared to authorise the marriage. Further information on marriage laws is available from the General Registry offices (see page 45).

Survival tactics

It may be great fun to hold the celebrations at your favourite museum, but make sure it has everything you need before you commit yourself to a booking. Check that it can handle any complications arising from your guest list.

Is it legal?

Ask the wedding coordinator about the legal requirements of being married at the site. Couples travelling overseas will need to verify the necessary documentation and check residency requirements for being married abroad with the embassy or tourism bureau. Double-check the requirements for religious and civil ceremonies and determine how much time is necessary to complete any paperwork.

Can it cater for all your needs?

Will you have exclusive rights to the entire location? If not, will the events coordinator at least provide a sense of privacy for your wedding? Does the location provide on-site catering? Is it suitable for children? Is there access to electricity and water? Are there adequate car-parking, cloakroom and powder-room or toilet facilities?

Finding answers to these and other questions at an early stage can avoid frustrations further down the line. It is good advice to visit the site in similar conditions to those you expect on your wedding day to imagine both the possibilities and the challenges. And if you intend for part or all of the festivities to be held outside, always consider alternatives in case of bad weather.

Get it in writing

As with every major aspect of your wedding, you'll want to enter into a contract with the venue, outlining the services that will be provided to you as well as your responsibilities. Usually, a 50 per cent deposit is required at the signing of such a contract, with the balance due on the wedding day.

Troublesome guests

Extended families that result from divorced parents can add an element of stress. Identify all the issues of concern and plan accordingly.

✳ Step-relatives may be anxious about feeling welcome. It is your job to play the chief peacemaker while trying not to get caught up in their politics.

✳ One solution for harmony on the wedding day is to be sure each parent is accompanied by a few of their close friends, who can serve as allies to boost their morale.

✳ If the guest list is getting out of hand, consider hosting a small wedding with the closest family members and friends, followed by a celebratory party with the larger circle of guests shortly after returning from the honeymoon.

Resources

Ceremony sites

www.noblesvenues.com
Noble's Wedding Venue Guides
A list of licensed civil wedding venues in
  England and Wales
The Noble Publishing Company
The Old Corn Store
Hawkhurst
Kent, TN18 5EU
Tel: 01580 752404

www.hitched.co.uk

The British Humanist Association
Tel: 020 7430 0908
(24-hour ceremony helpline 0870 516
  8122)

International Federation of Celebrants
www.celebrancy.com

Registration

Church of England
Tel: 020 7898 1000
www.cofe.anglican.org

Church of Scotland
Tel: 0131 225 5722
www.churchofscotland.org.uk

General Register Office for England and
  Wales
Tel: 0151 471 4200
www.groni.gov.uk

General Register Office for Guernsey
Tel: 01481 725277

General Register Office for Jersey
Tel: 01534 502335

General Register Office for Northern
  Ireland
Tel: 028 9025 2000

General Register Office for Scotland
Tel: 0131 314 4447
www.gro-scotland.gov.uk

Greek Archdiocese
Tel: 020 7723 4787

Jewish Marriage Council
Tel: 020 8203 6311

The London Buddhist Vihara
Tel: 020 8995 9493

Methodist Church
Tel: 020 7222 8010

United Reform Church
Tel: 020 7916 2020

Chapter Four
Planning The Reception

Party girls, get ready! Here's how to plan the biggest social event of the decade. The reception is the key to a perfect wedding day. It's where you get to indulge in every flight of fancy you ever dreamed of, from arriving in a Rolls Royce to dancing amid heart-shaped ice sculptures. Want something so fabulous that people are still talking about it in 20 years time? Here's where you'll find ideas for the ultimate wedding-day showstoppers.

The reception

It's really starting to happen. Feelings: yay and eek. Vineyard people have been v. helpful about reception style. And the freebies just keep coming. Jules told me you can get champagne-tastings and hors d'oeuvre samples and – you can! But got to stop. Am going to be huge before the (very) Big Day if do not get control of appetite.

Achieved so far:

Flowers

Met fabulous florist, recommended by hotel, last week. Her portfolio was amazing – she has done flowers for famous people, even one of the weddings in *Four Weddings*. . .

J loved meeting her as, with his gardening knowledge, he could spout Latin names all over place. It was v. easy to decide, once we'd seen a few pictures. It's going to be roses and ivy. Ivy all over stables, along ceiling and edge of tables, etc, with roses for bouquets, buttonholes and centrepieces.

Bit embarrassing when she asked me about my bouquet. My only opinion on this, previously (forgetting the embarrassing Dracula theme), had been that I didn't want one. Not really a very flowery person. But she understood, and we decided that it could look like these were just an armful of roses I'd picked on way to wedding. Like an innocent country girl. Quite like that picture of me. Better than a smoke-ridden old city journo, anyway.

Table decorations

Centre of tables: square glass vase filled with pebbles, with a single orchid growing out. HOW chic? Florist had one in corner of her apartment and J and I both loved it. And the pebble theme is really taking off: am going to have pebbles with guest's names painted on, as name cards. Rest of table will be simple elegance. Organisers have lots of little candles and holders we can use, so should be like twinkly grotto.

Food

Easy – we both picked our favourite meals. Lamb shank with mashed potatoes for me, salmon *en croute* for J. Two desserts: mini raspberry pavlova, and some chocolate cake thing that J chose. Starters – roasted-onion tartlets. Going to be SO delicious.

Dad also was total star and arranged for us to have constantly circulating trays of hors d'oeuvres. Said he was sick of going to weddings where there's no food for hours.

Drinks

Vineyard wine REALLY expensive. Not much cheaper to bring our own, as they charge corkage on every bottle. But anyway, we don't have to choose v. wide selection as there is paying bar there too. (Don't mind that – I've never resented paying for my own drinks at a wedding, as long as wine is free with meal. And there are men to buy me drinks. And a mini bar in my room.)

So, it's champagne and Buck's Fizz as we arrive. Then red and white for meal, champagne for toasts, and a bottle of cognac on every table for speeches. Oh, and cigars for the men.

Music

This was embarrassing, but J and I both want cheesy wedding disco. Like ones used to have when went to cousins' weddings as teenagers. The sort that play *Come on Eileen* to get everyone going, and *Lady In Red* to get everyone. . . er, really going. Vineyard representative swallowed a look of horror when we told him. But gave us a list and J made two calls and sorted it. DJ has even agreed to wear his worst Seventies corduroy suit to get even more cheesy. He'll start his set at 7.00 p.m., and end at midnight. Quite pleased it's a late one: want guests to have a good time at my wedding. Want lots of flirting and loads of gossip going on. (Maybe even babies made.)

Running order

Traditional. None of that modern "speeches before the meal" stuff. Everyone sits down at their places, J and I get announced and waltz in, we eat, then speeches, then coffee and cake. It was good enough for our parents. Etc. ✳

It's all in the planning

The reception is likely to be the first time you unwind from all the tensions of the last few days, even weeks. Careful organisation of this part of the wedding is essential if you are going to fully relax and enjoy yourself throughout the celebrations.

Since it follows directly on from the marriage ceremony, the style of the reception should complement and reflect your wedding theme as closely as possible. Typically, the costs involved for the reception represent about half the entire wedding budget. And while, traditionally, the financial responsibility of the reception falls to the parents of the bride, it is not unusual for couples to receive assistance from the groom's family as well or to assume some of the expenses themselves.

Wedding receptions can vary in style, size and location. Yours can be as simple as walking from the place of worship to a fellowship hall that's been decorated for the celebration, or as elaborate as travelling to a nearby setting, where a team of professional staff are at hand to execute the party of a lifetime. A private club or favourite restaurant might offer the feeling of being at home without any of the hassles, while a swanky hotel has the added convenience of accommodation for out-of-town guests.

After you confirm the availability of your chosen reception site by signing a contract and submitting a deposit, it's time to roll up your sleeves and get on with the details.

Transportation

One of the last worries that you'll want to have on your wedding day is that one of the bridesmaids can't find your house, or that a few of the groom's attendants get lost driving between the ceremony and the reception.

With a little pre-planning of wedding day transportation, you can be sure that all of the wedding party are exactly where they need to be and on time. Your budget may allow for a fleet of limousines to carry you and your bridesmaids, the groom and his men, and the parents and grandparents from place to place. If not, think about friends who drive large sedans or minivans that might be willing to play chauffeur for you. Do you know of a vintage car that might be available to you? (Or a horse and carriage?)

Transportation arrangements will probably be sorted by your fiancé, but sit down together first and write the following three lists to make sure everyone in the wedding party is catered for:

✱ Your pick-up location and time, plus the list of passengers who will ride with you to the ceremony.

Something less conventional?

● How about both of you arriving on a tandem? Or a Harley Davidson?

● Hire an open-top bus so that everyone goes from A to B to C together– accompanied by a case of chilled champagne.

● Investigate the practicalities (and costs) of being transported by a riverboat, helicopter or classic sports car.

✱ The groom's pick-up location and time, plus the list of passengers who will ride with him to the ceremony.

✱ The location of the ceremony and time to depart for the reception, plus the list of all the VIPs who need transportation.

All out-of-town guests should be provided with maps and driving directions to all of the key wedding spots. You might ask family friends to help escort guests who have travelled a significant distance to your wedding and aren't familiar with the sites.

Finally, you'll want to be sure that your honeymoon getaway from the reception site is properly planned (something else your man should be sorting). Give him a nudge and hint that you've always imagined the pair of you in a sports car – not one with a "Just Married" sign in the back window and a streamer of tin cans tied to the rear bumper, but one that you get to keep.

Wedding flowers

With about ten per cent of the wedding budget allocated for flowers, it's important to secure (well in advance) a professional florist you can relate to – someone who understands what you want and can work within that budget. Seek recommendations from family and friends, and interview each candidate to determine who has the creative flair that works for you.

It is most practical to start with your dress and those of your bridesmaids as a basis for colour scheme and style. Your bouquet should be considered an accessory to your dress, not too large and not too small. The style of your dress might influence what type of bouquet would look best – whether a nosegay, cascade or arm bouquet – or if a single flower would create a more dramatic image. You may also choose to wear flowers tucked into your hair. The buttonholes for the men and corsages for the women should tie in with your theme too.

An established florist will likely be familiar with the locations for your ceremony and reception and can advise you how floral accents can enhance the settings. Most churches and synagogues require very little decoration beyond simple arrangements at the altar and to mark pews for the family and wedding party. Some brides marrying in a Jewish ceremony will choose a *chuppah*, or wedding canopy, embellished with flowers. Check with the wedding director at the church or synagogue to learn of any guidelines or restrictions related to the decorations.

At the reception, flowers can be used to trim the surroundings as well as enhance the table settings. You can have a tiny vase at each place setting, or place a larger arrangement at the centre of the table. Be sure that the height of the centrepiece is either below or above the eye level of the guests around the table so as not to obstruct views or conversation. Doorways, stairway rails, fireplace mantels or windowsills all present opportunities for floral accents.

Particular things to consider (which your florist will be able to advise on) are flowers that will be in season when you get married; should/can any of the blooms be scented; and whether you will be able to save money by transferring the flowers from the ceremony on to the reception. Find out whether your florist can be there on the day to make this possible.

Something different

You don't have to stop at convention when you consider your arrangements:

❋ Bouquets, garlands and table displays can be striking when made of green foliage, woody stems and berries.

❋ Combine flowers with pebbles, shells or beads, metals, candles and glass to complement your wedding theme.

❋ Collect offered flower stems from the female guests as you enter the ceremony for a more natural look.

❋ Opt for moss, mini-topiary, bonsai or cacti for a super-stylish affair or have goldfish in bowls as centrepieces for your tables.

❋ Don't forget that fruit and vegetables, such as artichokes, asparagus, pumpkins and citrus fruit can all be used to dramatic effect.

Wedding music

There is no limit to the music you can have at the reception –
except, perhaps, space. Choose well, and you will be able to create
the perfect ambience for the day as well as providing a vehicle for
the entertainment.

Often, the size of the audience determines the best type of music, with a small ensemble best suited for a more intimate gathering and a mini-orchestra for a larger crowd. Another option that works best all round is a disc jockey who plays a selection of your favourite records.

To begin planning the best music for your reception, start by identifying the budget you can lay out for it and research the bands or musicians that will fit in with your scheme. Next, assess the size and layout of the reception venue to establish the level of sound that is necessary to entertain the guests but not overpower the goings-on.

Ask around for references from people who have hired or heard reception musicians and who are also familiar with your tastes and sense of style. Look for professionals who have ample experience, and who can relate to your vision of the party. Try to ascertain each band's depth of musical repertoire and their flexibility in satisfying any special requests.

Once you have selected the musical group for your reception, make plans to collaborate on the list of song titles to be played. Provide the bandleader with an agenda of the reception events, and develop a contract to confirm the date and time of the event along with the number of musicians who will perform, appropriate attire for the players, the fee and the arrangement for overtime.

Be specific about your song preferences and the scheduling of the bride and groom's first dance, the bride's dance with her father and the groom's dance with his mother, the toasts, the cutting of the cake, and the last dance before you and the groom leave for the honeymoon.

From a musical perspective, think about your wedding reception in two or three segments:

✱ First will be a pre-meal hour when guests mingle over cocktails or hors d'oeuvres. The music should serve as a backdrop for conversation – a string quartet or a jazz trio perhaps.

✱ Next is the meal hour, where a variety of tunes that appeal to all of the guests is best. You can opt for a selection of pre-recorded songs, have a solo singer or continue with your pre-meal choice.

✱ Lively dancing typically follows the meal, and here you can have anything from a classic big band sound to karaoke, depending on your wedding theme.

Food and drink

When deciding on the type of food service that you want to offer your family members and friends, you'll want to take into account the time of day and the venue for the celebration along with the style you want for your reception.

What are your options?

* A morning affair calls for breakfast or brunch – omelettes or eggs Benedict, waffles or crepes, fresh fruit and pastries.

* An early day celebration begs for salads and light entrées.

* Miniature sandwiches and bite-sized titbits suit an afternoon tea.

* Opt for a picnic or barbecue for a more informal daytime meal.

* Afternoon or evening celebrations are also perfect for a cocktail reception with hot and cold hors d'oeuvres presented as a buffet or passed by waiters.

* An evening function requires a substantial dinner-like menu, perhaps served in several courses.

Depending on the number of guests you are having, you can decide to do the catering yourself (with help from the family), to use the staff available at the venue or engage an outside caterer. Discuss the kind of menu you want and ask for a few suggestions to choose from. All caterers should offer a tasting session where you can make a final selection from a number of dishes. (Remember to include a vegetarian or ingredient-intolerant option if required.)

Having the caterer or the venue provide the drinks is an easy option, but can often end up being more expensive, particularly if you have an open bar. If you are lucky to live within driving distance of a wholesale supplier or, better still, a vineyard, you can purchase wine and beer at considerably lower prices.

The wedding cake

This is one of the oldest wedding traditions, and is something else that can reflect the theme of your wedding. Traditionally the cake is a three-tiered, rich, moist cake with icing, but in recent years there has been a move to vary the style of the cake.

These days, you can opt for whatever shape cake appeals to you – a person, a building, a work of art – and the flavour, filling and icing can be a combination of anything you like. Your choice here is unlimited, but be careful, as this has led to brides requesting the impossible. Some of the most popular pairings are pound cake with butter cream icing, carrot cake with

cream cheese icing, and chocolate cake with white chocolate icing.

Aim to have a pretty good idea of what you want before you start looking for a baker. That way you are more likely to end up with something close to your plan, and can quickly eliminate those that are not up to the task. Gather together pictures from magazines and look on the Internet for ideas, and always be prepared to take advice from the baker as well. If you get really stuck, head to the store that makes the tastiest cakes in town and see if they can offer you direction.

Top layer tradition

If you are following convention, make arrangements for the top layer of the wedding cake to be frozen after the reception and stored until the naming ceremony of your first child.

Photography

The photographer is probably the single most important professional to take part in a wedding. He or she is charged with capturing all the events of the day and plays a large part in scheduling and organising the sequence of those events.

For this reason alone you should put your faith behind a recommended professional when it comes to preserving the Big Day on film. The best are in high demand, so you'll want to hire yours asap, even up to a year in advance. Ask your friends for recommendations, and make notes of the photographers' names in wedding magazines. Schedule face-to-face interviews, and ask to see sample albums to get an idea of the photographer's style. Discuss his or her fee structure, the payment schedule for the deposit and final balance, and a timetable of when to expect your proofs and the final album.

Once you've found a photographer that shares the same vision as you, provide him or her with a written copy of all the details of the wedding, including the schedule of the day, the number and names of the wedding party, and sticky situations that may require special care. Talk about your preference for posed as well as candid shots and the layout for the album that will ultimately be created.

Mix it up

You don't have to go for one style of photography over another. Sure, hire the pro to take posed shots of you and your (now) husband with family and friends after the ceremony – these will likely be the images that stand the test of time. But go for reportage shots too: have friends circulate a Polaroid camera or place disposable cameras on the tables at the reception. With a mixture of colour and black-and-white film, you'll get the formality of the day combined with the relaxed ambience of the occasion.

Videography

A video can capture moments that printed photography can't. Just like searching for your photographer, start to interview videographers early on. Ask to view samples and pay attention to how the cameraman moves from scene to scene in anticipation of the upcoming event. Make sure the cameraman has a steady hand and that the imagery is in sharp focus.

Describe the details of your wedding along with the theme that you are trying to instill. Be sure to book enough time, perhaps starting with you both individually dressing for the wedding, through the ceremony and reception until you leave for the honeymoon. Discuss music that can be used on your tape, and whether you want the videographer to invite guests to offer special congratulations to the two of you.

66 We hired a local amateur to take a mixture of posed and reportage shots throughout our wedding. On the day, however, it was obvious he was way out of his depth. He was neither commanding enough to assemble groups for posed shots, nor did he have the confidence to act the paparazzo. It was a disaster, with our worst suspicions confirmed when he sent us the results. I wish we'd gone for a professional now. 99 **Olivia, 24**

Reception etiquette

There are a number of conventions that take place at the reception: a traditional seating plan, speechmaking, the first dance and tossing the bouquet are some of them. It is entirely up to you whether you choose to incorporate them into your wedding day.

The pros and cons of a receiving line

You may well balk at the idea of having a receiving line at your wedding, but there is no argument that it's the best way to greet every guest. Nevertheless, at a large wedding, this can take up a tremendous amount of time. For some weddings, having a receiving line will seem way too formal. So why go through with it?

The purpose is simple: it allows every guest to express his or her best wishes to the newlyweds and congratulations to their parents. According to tradition, this should happen at the ceremony site as your guests embark for the reception. However, it makes sense to stage the receiving line at the entrance to the reception; alternatively you may prefer to position the line inside so that you can offer drinks and hors d'oeuvres to guests as they wait their turn.

As the hostess of the reception, the mother of the bride heads the receiving line. The mother of the groom, and the bride and groom, follow her. Since most fathers would prefer to circulate among the guests, they may be excused from the receiving line to make sure that all of the guests are enjoying themselves.

If the chief bridesmaid and best man are family members, they should be included at the end; if they are professional chums who don't know many of the guests, they should not. Some couples place a guest register at the end of the receiving line to be assured that every guest will have an opportunity to sign the book.

What's the alternative? If you decide against it, you should allow enough time at the beginning of the reception for the newlyweds and the parents to circulate among the guests, making an effort to speak to everyone.

The seating plan

Decisions over your seating plan will be influenced by the layout of the reception site and the number of guests you have invited. Traditionally, the newlyweds sit at the centre of a long table that faces the rest of the guests, and are flanked on either side by the remaining members of the wedding party. Alternatives to this arrangement are for the parents of the bride and groom to be seated together, hosting a table of their own and joined by family and close friends.

A new reception trend is for the bride and groom to be seated at a small, decorated table for two to celebrate their first meal together, surrounded by tables of their wedding party members.

Plan for a table to be placed near the entrance to the reception room that will alphabetically list each guest and his or her allocated table name or number. The most formal wedding celebration also calls for place cards to identify which seat a guest takes at each table.

Toasts and speechmaking

One of the most sentimental and historic of wedding customs is the wedding toast. It's the best man's responsibility to take centre stage as soon as guests are comfortably seated at the reception and presented with something to drink, or alternatively just before the newlyweds cut the cake.

Champagne is the popular choice for toasting. If the crowd is large, use a microphone so that everyone can hear what is said. At the end of his speech, the best man proposes a toast and the guests raise their glasses. The bride and groom should remain seated and smile in appreciation of the good wishes.

The groom should then step forward to thank the best man for his kind words, and offer a toast to his new wife, his new in-laws and his own parents. If the bride cares to, she can offer a toast next, first to her new husband and then to the parents. Any other guests or friends are welcome to rise and offer a toast to the newlyweds.

It is up to you whether you follow tradition or not. If the best man is cripplingly shy or your Mum wants to make the big speech, so be it. There are bound to be people who are itching to say a few words and you should let them. You could always have a few poems read out instead of speeches.

The first dance

Whether at the beginning of the reception, or as the music restarts after the meal, there will come the time when you both take to the centre of the dance floor for your first steps as husband and wife.

If you are committed to this, but cannot dance, you may want to take professional lessons early on or at least practise until you can move smoothly together. Your choice of song may be a sentimental classic or may have been a popular tune when you were dating or became engaged. It should have a slow to medium beat to allow you to dance effortlessly in your wedding gown.

"" My brother and sister-in-law broke all the rules when they got married last year and asked their chief bridesmaid to give the main speech. And because Susie had no pressure to follow in the tradition of best-man-speak, she was able to deliver some fantastic lines – funny yet respectful, emotional but not sentimental. It was the most moving wedding speech I have ever heard and I was really proud for all of them. "" **Kate, 36**

I hated every minute of our first dance. It seemed to go on for ever and we both felt pretty awkward. It certainly wasn't the romantic schmooze we had both practised beforehand. The bandleader realised, completely changed the tempo, and joined us on the dance floor. He really saved the day! **Marilyn, 27**

Usually, the couple will dance alone to the entire song before any cut-ins. Most often, the music changes to another chosen melody as the bride dances with her father and the groom with his mother. As that song comes to a close, her father invites his mother to dance so that the bride can dance with her new father-in-law and the groom can dance with his new mother-in-law. If any parent is without a partner, pair him or her with an appropriate relative or friend.

After the parents' dance, the bridal party will be invited to join in a special dance before all of the guests are called to the dance floor.

Alternatives to this custom are for the bride and groom to take to the floor for the first few minutes of the dance – so that pictures can be taken – and for the rest of the wedding party to join in shortly after. If the idea of the first dance is something that fills you with horror, you can of course do away with it altogether or make it the real "last dance" of the evening before you make your honeymoon exit.

Tossing the bouquet

The gathering of the single, female guests at the reception often signals the nearing of the end of the celebrations as the bride turns her back to the crowd and pitches the bouquet over her head. For brides choosing to preserve their wedding-day flowers, consider ordering a "toss" bouquet from your florist to use for this festivity. It can be a detailed miniature of your real bouquet or a simple cluster of your favourite flowers tied with pretty ribbon.

The honeymoon getaway

The bride and groom are traditionally the first to leave the reception, applauded by guests tossing rice, flower petals or forming an archway as the newlyweds depart for their honeymoon. There is nothing to stop couples staying for the entire duration of the party should they wish to, but tell guests your plan so that they do not stay longer than they wish to themselves, waiting to send you off formally.

Making a difference

Your wedding will be remembered by the elements that make it personal to you, and to that end there are special touches (and outright showstoppers) that you can incorporate in both the marriage service and the celebration that follows.

Special touches

✳ For the service, design a programme that identifies members of the wedding party and lists each part of the ceremony. The style of the programme should follow the same design theme as your invitations, and can be passed out by the ushers as they seat the guests on arrival at the ceremony.

✳ During the ceremony, you may choose to include the tradition of the unity candle that symbolises the joining of two individuals.

✳ At the reception, plan to present a bomboniere at each place setting, ranging from a tiny frame with a photo of the two of you, to a bundle of sugared almonds wrapped in tulle, or a packet of flower seeds to commemorate the beginning and growth of your marriage.

✳ Chocolate wrappers with your picture and the date, a compact disc of your favourite love songs or a jigsaw puzzle are some of the more unique alternatives.

✳ Move away from the traditional throwing of rice and confetti and instead use flower petals, potpourri or bubbles.

✳ As you leave the reception, have your guests stand along both sides of the exit path holding burning sparklers for a glistening send-off or organise a dazzling firework display.

Showstoppers

✳ Make an impact by arriving by boat or helicopter (venue permitting).

✳ Release white doves or butterflies at the completion of the ceremony.

✳ Announce the completion of your ceremony in sky writing.

✳ If your celebrations are taking place by the coast, make a weekend of it and have a day on the beach with your guests.

✳ Hire a group of magicians and performers to mingle among the crowd as the reception kicks off.

✳ Hire a celebrity musician for the evening reception.

✳ Hire a snow machine for real snowflakes at a winter celebration.

Bridal registry

Thanks to the bridal registry services at department and speciality stores, you can have a gift list that is all taken care of in one place. You'll be able to choose anything you want for the dining room, kitchen, bedrooms and bathrooms, as well as accessories for entertaining, sports or the garden.

For couples that have either lived on their own for a while or perhaps lived together before the wedding and have already accumulated many of the everyday items for their home, the bridal registry may seem less important. In such cases it makes more sense to ask for the money. However, asking for money is considered poor taste. Instead, have your parents and attendants inform inquiring guests that you'd be especially grateful to receive gifts of vouchers or cash that would be used towards a major purchase or deposit on a house.

Want to be less conventional?
If you already have the domestic baggage to last a lifetime (and are happy with it), here are a few ideas for an alternative wish list:

✱ Tickets to a sporting match, the theatre, an exhibition or a gig.

✱ Vouchers for your favourite store, restaurant, theme park, garden nursery.

✱ A case of wine, champagne, virgin olive oil or your favourite perfume(s).

✱ Contributions to your music, cacti or vodka collection.

✱ Pets: a fluffy kitten, an aged tortoise or 20 tropical fish.

✱ A bag of luxury goodies for the honeymoon journey.

❝ We found an easy solution to our gift list and decided to replace older gadgets with new-improved ones. A few weeks before the wedding we picked out our stuff and went to a car boot sale. This way we were able to pocket extra cash for the honeymoon and redecorate our home with brand-new gifts at the same time. ❞
Jackie, 37

Survival tactics

You are going to be hiring a good number of professionals over the next few months – a photographer, a florist, a baker, a stationer, musicians, caterers and more. Simply coordinating them will be a task in itself and there are ways of making your life easier.

✱ Always do your homework. Look through magazines, trawl the Internet, ask friends and family for recommendations. Before even picking up the phone, have a very clear idea of the look, sound, flavour of whatever it is you are asking for.

✱ Ask to see examples of previous work, certificates or proof of qualifications, commendations from happy customers, newspaper or magazine articles – anything that confirms you are getting the level of expertise you want.

✱ Do not underestimate advice you might get from a pro, however. These are the people with the experience and it would be a bad thing if they had nothing to contribute to your ideas.

✱ Keep a close eye on your budget and stick to it. Be up front with all professionals from the very beginning. Do not be persuaded to increase your budget unless it is for something simply amazing.

✱ Agree to a realistic timeframe. Check out other commitments your suppliers may have and make sure they are not going to interfere with yours.

✱ Get everything in writing, confirming who is to do what, by when, and include a payment schedule.

Resources

Wedding favours

Charming Weddings
5 Talybont Grove
Ingleby Barwick
Stockton-on Tees, TS17 5EH
Tel: 01642 769279,
www.weddingwinecharmfavours.co.uk

'I do' Wedding Favours
Bournestream
Silian
Lampeter, SA48 8AX
Tel: 01570 423262
www.idoweddingfavours.co.uk

Paper Lace
29 South Street
Dalkeith
Midlothian, EH22 1AH
Tel: 0131 663 2491
www.weddingfavours.co.uk

Caterers/marquees etc

Cresta Caterers
35 Aberaman Park Industrial Estate
Aberdare, CF44 6DA
Tel: 01685 876111
www.crestacaterers.co.uk

The London Marquee Company
5 Beechmore Road
London, SW11 4ET
Tel: 020 7610 1770
 www.marqueecelebrations.co.uk

Photography

British Institute of Professional
  Photography
Fox Talbot House
Ware, SG12 9HN
Tel: 01920 464011
www.bipp.com

Guild of Wedding Photographers
59 Fore Street
Trowbridge
Wiltshire, BA14 8ET
Tel: 0161 926 9367
www.gwp-uk.co.uk

Association of Professional Videomakers
Ambler House
Helpringham
Lincolnshire, NG34 0RB
Tel: 01529 421717
www.apv.org.uk

Wedding flowers

Miraflores Limited
Tel: 0800 138 2820
www.miraflores.org.uk
www.bridalflowers.co.uk
www.confetti.co.uk
www.weddingflorist.co.uk

Wedding music

Music for London
15-19 Upper Montagu Street
London W1H 2PQ
Tel: 020 7724 1917
www.musicforlondon.co.uk

The Wedding Music Company
144 Greenwich High Street
London SE10 8NN
Tel: 020 8293 3392
www.weddingmusic.co.uk

www.weddingmanual.co.uk

Chapter Five
What To Wear (And How)

So the venue's sorted, the invitations are being written and your theme is finally decided. All you need to think about now is what you are going to wear on the most important day of your life. This is where some brides are more fortunate than others, having spent their teenage years designing wedding dresses on the backs of schoolbooks. If you weren't one of those girls – or even if you were – you're going to need to source a dress, shoes and hairstyle to inspire admiration, and perhaps a little envy, in everyone.

The dress

Surfed Internet today in search of second-hand wedding dress. Had to really — our budget is blown and there's no way I can afford a new one. Can't believe how expensive they are. Even the most hideous off-the-peg dresses are about £1,500. Am I missing something? You do just wear it for one day, right?

Not that going to the shops was all bad; assistants are lovely, everyone is v. happy, and you get free coffee. Even someone else's Mum got teary when I emerged in one dress. (Not that mine did. She was at home watching daytime telly — said I was hell to shop with.) Might have helped if someone had warned me to wear my best underwear, though. I was in my worst — ripped tights, grey, holey knickers, and no bra (blush). Assistants were in and out of the changing room like mad things. "How are you getting on?" they'd shout seconds after giving me a dress to put on, tearing the curtain wide open so everyone could see my all.

So, the Internet. Found a brilliant site where real-life brides post photos of their wedding alongside an advert for the dress. So funny. Too funny, in cruel way. The photos were hilarious (where did they find those grooms? Ick!) but the best bits were their comments. "Everyone said I looked beautiful in my dress", wrote one. They had lied.

Got v. organised in the afternoon and bought a wedding magazine for ideas. So hard to choose. Maybe if I'd been more romantic as a teenager I'd have planned everything long ago. I wasn't. Never thought I would ever get long-term boyfriend, let alone husband. So now feel woefully unprepared. And all bridal models seem stick-thin. Of course they'd look good in tight shiny white satin, but can't help thinking I'd look like a blimp. But in back of mag was advert for local woman who sells second-hand dresses.

Paid a visit after work. Brilliant! Room full of dresses all hung up over walls. Racks and racks. Everything. And all worn just the once, so perfect condition. (Can't help thinking mine won't be though, bound to be covered in wine, grass stains, tears and worse — and that's just on way to service.) Tried on loads, until…

I FOUND THE DRESS. It is so perfect. Ivory duchess satin (whatever that means), full-length in two pieces. Corset top, with ties round back and chiffon sleeves. (Essential as naked, my arms look like bat wings.) Skirt is full length, sort of A-line, with petticoats. Heaven! Made woman tie ribbons so tight almost fainted. But boobs look great. Satin so smooth that I have two boobs visible, instead of the one long bolster I had in other dresses.

Even the woman said it suited me. (And she wasn't a woman given to meaningless praise.) In fact, she had already told me that I should "do something about that hair" and "lose a few kilos before Big Day". What was with her? So different to fawning assistants in bridal shops. Was she bitter jilted woman committed to heaping misery on young brides? Or am I just fat cow with bad hair? Hmm.

Despite her weight comment, it fits perfectly. And is half its original (designer's naturally) price. As is so gorgeous I won't need any jewellery. All need to get is boots. I'm thinking crushed velvet, dark blue, with pointy toe. Gothic-style. And bridesmaids can wear dark-blue dresses. (Really wish had guts to put them into fuschia Crimplene ra-ra dresses, like threaten to when drunk.)

But my dress. It's soooo perfect. My only fear is superstition – what if woman who wore it first time is divorced already? (Dress is year old, apparently.) What if dress is made from unlucky, cursed satin, woven by jilted witch? What if whoever wears it is doomed to die alone?

Dress is so sexy, even if J doesn't show up, someone else'll marry me. I do look very good in it. Who'd have thought? Shall have to get married lots of times. ✳

What's your style?

Many modern brides start off determined to wear anything but a white gown on the Big Day, yet find themselves drawn in that direction once they start looking for something.

The outfit you choose for the Big Day may well depend on the size and style of the occasion. The more formal the wedding, the closer you will get to the full-length, all-frills gown. But don't be put off wearing a dress altogether if a traditional look is not your style. First off, the dress does not have to be white (or any shade of cream through ivory for that matter). There are pastel options ranging from subtle blues and pinks to cappuccino brown, lilac and pistachio. For a richer, more luxuriant look, consider navy, emerald, scarlet or burgundy velvet. Brides looking for the ultimate fairytale look can even select from a range of metallics, starting with gold and silver, but also shimmery blues and pinks.

There is also hope for brides who hesitate at the idea of swathes of satin, embroidered bodices and three-metre trains, as your choice of dress style is inexhaustible – particularly if you *do* see yourself wearing white. A wedding dress does not have to be complicated in design, neither does it have to be full length. Depending on your size and shape (see page 70) you can opt for soft flowing lines or something skimpy, fresh and fun. Consider wearing a suit and not a dress, and you get to mix and match style

and colour too. Instead of heavy brocade have fun with beads, sequins, sew-on butterflies or flowers.

If you are still unsure, why not look to your wedding theme for inspiration (see page 20).

* A hot summer wedding might call for a simple-cut floral dress for a country setting, or a batik-style mini-sundress for an on-the-beach affair, or a natty pantsuit for a ceremony on board a cruise ship or yacht.

* The colder months suggest soft, warm velvets for a winter celebration, vintage costume for a Victorian theme and a combination of earthy tones for a wedding in autumn.

> 66 I knew from the start that I wanted to wear deep-red satin and it took some time to convince my Mum (and his). We kept it a secret from my fiancé and now, five years on, Peter still insists that the highlight of his day was seeing me for the first time. 99
>
> **Lucy, 37**

The bridesmaids' attire

There's an age-old joke about all the expensive but hideous bridesmaids' dresses that one can accumulate as your friends lose their otherwise high taste for fashion and succumb to momentary bridal mania.

Though true in some cases (when a bridesmaid can console herself in vain that there will be another perfect occasion someday that she can wear the dress), it doesn't have to go this way. While there is a tradition for all bridesmaids to wear the same style dress, regardless of size or skin tone, it is no longer practised at all weddings, and there are a number of alternatives available to the modern bride.

What are your options?

* If you have bridesmaids of a similar size and shape, you can opt for the same style dress, but have each maid in a different colour or tone to complement your own.

* After determining some basic parameters, like length and formality, you might choose a theme colour and have each attendant find a dress style in that colour that she really likes and that suits her.

* For a stylish evening reception, the bridesmaids could each choose their own little black dress, and complete the look with coordinated accessories.

* If a favourite shop has a seasonal collection, your bridesmaids can buy an outfit each from the coordinating skirts, blouses and dresses.

* Vintage weddings can be real fun, with all of you shopping together for genuine outfits that capture perfectly the era of your theme.

If you are having the dresses made, you'll want to start shopping at least six months in advance to allow plenty of time for delivery and any alterations that might need to be made. Your chief bridesmaid is responsible for collecting the measurements of each maid and organising the order. However, it is down to each woman to be brutally honest in providing her personal numbers, since the sizing of bridal attire is not the same as ready-to-wear fashions and they will otherwise end up with an outfit that clearly doesn't fit them properly.

Each one will need to put down a deposit when her dress is ordered and should pay the balance when they pick it up. Alterations are typically included in the prices offered at full-service boutiques, except in the case of sale dresses, where there is an added charge.

Customarily, the bridesmaids pay for their own dresses plus matching shoes. This can amount to a considerable expense – even more so once accessories have been added to the shopping list – and you would do well to bear this in mind when deciding on a style for your bridesmaids. In cases where the shoes won't show under a floor-length gown, the bride may choose a basic style of shoe she prefers and let each maid make her own purchase, accepting they will not all be exactly the same in design.

Matching jewellery, given as a gift by the bride, accentuates the gown and lowers the costs for each of her bridesmaids. For a traditional look, bridesmaids should wear the same jewellery, but none should wear a watch on the day.

What shape are you?

Before doing anything, be completely honest with yourself and the mirror in recognising your best and worst features. Most brides opt for some kind of dress and you'll want one that accentuates your good attributes but minimises the bits you are not so happy with.

Short

Good: gowns that have vertical lines or decoration to give the illusion of height; a hat wrapped with tulle as a showstopper accessory.

Not so good: heavy fabrics and those with complex ornamentation.

Tall

Good: gowns with sophisticated and sweeping lines; any major horizontal design elements at the shoulder or the waistline, which will minimise height; decorative detailing to the neckline or hemline; any satin and linen fabrics.

Not so good: gowns with vertical lines or decoration.

Large bust

Good: an off-the-shoulder dress or one with an open, shaped neckline; a fitted waistline or low-cut back to draw the eye away from your bosom.

Not so good: a high neckline; a high waistline; elaborate detailing on the bodice.

Small bust

Good: loose, fitted bodice with high neck and covered shoulders; a deep v- or scoop back; full, embellished skirt with detailed fabrication or special hem interest.

Not so good: a tight bodice or open neckline; any necklace.

Slim

Good: a fitted style paired with full, gathered skirt or horizontal detailing at the waistline; a neckline, skirt or decorative sleeves that call attention away from your mid-section.

Not so good: a narrow skirt; an exaggerated waistline; puffed sleeves.

Slim waistline

Good: a dress that makes the most of your curvaceous figure; a gown with a fitted waist and decorated bodice; an off-the-shoulder neckline and softly gathered skirt.

Not so good: any style with decoration on both bodice and skirt, or with a horizontal design detail at the waist.

Full figure

Good: lightweight fabrics with matte finishes; V-necks, keyhole or scoop necklines; fitted sleeves; empire waists and A-line silhouettes; earrings or an headpiece to bring attention to the face.

Not so good: bulky fabrics like velvet or heavy satin; glossy fabrics; puffed or full sleeves; large back bow; pouf veil.

Full waistline

Good: an off-the-shoulder design or one with an empire waist; a deep or open neckline to call attention upwards; an elongated waistline and fancy skirt to call attention downwards.

Not so good: any type of detail at the waist or a heavily embellished bodice.

Pear-shaped

Good: a gentle princess line will create a slimming effect; a decorative bodice with a scoop- or V-neck to draw attention upwards.

Not so good: any detailing at the waistline; a full, embellished skirt; any decorative trimming along the hemline.

Unshapely arms

Good: cover up with the perfect sleeve; a shaped neckline; a decorative bodice.

Not so good: sleeveless, off-the-shoulder or halter styles.

Shapely legs

Good: a short, above-the-knee skirt; a sheath with a side slit.

Not so good: a billowing, ball-gown skirt.

Dark-skinned

Good: white fabrics or pale pastel tones.

Not so good: ivory colorations with yellow undertones.

Fair-skinned

Good: warm naturals and various ivory colours.

Not so good: stark white, which tends to wash out pale skin tones.

Long neck

Good: round neckline; detailing at waist or skirt; simple headband, crescent or cap with fingertip or longer veil.

Not so good: high neck or collar; any necklace or dangling earrings.

Short hair

Good: dramatic earrings; handband or crescent headpiece; floral wereath handband or halo.

Not so good: diminutive earrings, cap-style headpice, tiara or crown.

Long hair

Good: chignon or upswept hairstyle; side hair pulled back from face and affixed with decorative combs or back bow.

Not so good: danglng earrings; unkempt hairstyle.

Buying your gown

You'll probably put a day aside for visiting bridal boutiques or your favourite department stores to find something you like and can afford. Don't be surprised if that day turns into a multiple of days before the perfect dress is found.

With this in mind it makes sense to get started on the hunt for your dress as soon as you have decided the type of wedding you want. A four- to six-month lead time is advised for ordering a dress and having it custom-fitted before the Big Day.

Know what you want
It is best to get some ideas before you shop and a good place to start is by looking at every bridal magazine you can get your hands on. Photographs of wedding gowns dominate the pages, and you'll be able to spot the latest trends. Pick out the styles that you like, and take pictures with you. Maybe you are wild about just one detail rather than the entire style of a dress – take that with you too.

Make an appointment at a full-service boutique, where you can enlist the aid of an experienced bridal consultant who has assisted numerous brides before you. Describe the wedding that you are planning, and let her know the budget you are working with for your gown and accessories. Show her pictures of gowns that you admire, and then ask her to show you examples that she thinks will meet all of your criteria. You will be trying dresses

At the bridal salon

- Remember to take the undergarments and shoes you plan to wear on the day.

- See how different shades of white enhance your skin tone; there is a broad range of colour between white and ivory, and you should choose the most flattering shade.

- If you are planning on losing some weight between choosing your dress and the wedding, be sure to let the bridal consultant know up front. Discuss ways in which this may influence the style of dress you choose.

- Examine the interior construction of each dress to determine the quality of workmanship. Are the seams sewn straight? Are the decorative details securely attached? Is the overall workmanship acceptable?

- Try on several dresses with trains of varying lengths to realise how the weight of the back will feel during the marriage ceremony. (The boutique can design a bustle for the train to help you move with ease at the reception, or look at styles with a removable train.)

- Discuss your accessories (see pages 74–75).

- Make an appointment for a first fitting as soon as you have chosen your dress, and an appointment for a final fitting two weeks before the wedding for any last-minute changes.

- You should be prepared to place a 50 per cent deposit when you order your dress with the balance due when you pick it up after the final fitting.

on, so wear appropriate underwear and arrange your hair similarly to the way you plan to wear it on your wedding day (see page 76).

Bride on a budget

Not every bride will consider her gown to be the most important facet of the wedding, and would prefer to see the money going elsewhere. Luckily, there are lots of suitable options for every style and bank balance.

Your first stop might be a consignment shop that carries once-worn bridal gowns. Take note that while you may be able to buy the dress very inexpensively, you will have to find a talented dressmaker who can fit the dress perfectly to your figure.

Look out for bridal salon sales of sample dresses or discontinued styles. The boutique might provide the alterations and professional cleaning of a sale dress for an additional charge.

If someone in your family is a dressmaker, you could have your dream dress for an affordable fee.

Preserving your gown

The job of preserving a wedding gown should be entrusted only to a professional. Although your favourite dry cleaner has performed miracles on many of your outfits in the past, the task is best directed to a specialist who is trained in treating highly delicate fabrics with embellished details.

To the naked eye, your dress may appear in great shape, but in reality it's been soiled by perspiration, champagne, wine and countless other substances that will, untreated, break down the fabric of the gown as well as stain it. You need a professional who can deal with the soiling without damaging the materials.

At the same time, you'll want to have the gown wrapped in acid-free paper and packed for storage in an acid-free box. Avoid an airtight container, as mould may develop, or a window box, since the biggest enemy to your dress is light. Once complete, store the box at a moderate temperature where it won't be subject to either overheating or extreme cold.

Finishing touches

You are going to be the centre of attention for the whole day. While your dress will certainly be the main focus, it is the accessories that will be working together to complete the look successfully.

Headpieces

Any headpiece should flatter the shape of your face and blend with your hairstyle. It may be made of the same fabric as your gown, made of a similar material or be designed around a tiara. Most bridal gowns take on a classier look with the addition of a veil, which can range in length from elbow- or fingertip-length to the longest, three-metre cathedral veil. Often, a headpiece is constructed with a removable veil that allows you to move freely after the marriage service. For a less traditional look, you may opt for a hat or simply wear flowers in your hair. Look through bridal magazines for ideas and for contact details of individual designers should you want to commission something specific.

Jewellery

The fabric and decorative detail of your gown will dictate the type of jewellery you wear. Pearls have been the classic favourite gem in bridal jewellery for years, and are now being updated with the addition of sparkling rhinestones.

Dresses with an open neckline will beg for either a necklace with tiny earrings, or just some elaborate, dangling earrings. Sleeveless or short-sleeve styles may be enhanced with a bracelet that can be worn alone or over long white gloves. Find a pretty silver or gold anklet to wear with a dress that has a short skirt. If your gown has a high neck and long sleeves, the only extra jewellery you'll want will be some delicate earrings.

Lingerie

Under your gown, you'll need the very best foundations to help your dress sit on your body smoothly and comfortably. A full skirt will need some kind of underskirt for support, and this can either be attached to the inside of the gown or worn as an independent item.

If you are the lucky recipient of the gift of lingerie at your engagement party or on your hen night, you will now surely have the perfect lacy bra and knickers to wear on the day. For bridal hosiery, you can choose anything from fine denier silk stockings to lacy knit tights and those with patterned motifs. Most of these will be available in varying shades of white to match your dress or outfit.

Shoes

As you shop for shoes, remember that you will spend most of your wedding day on

Think accessories

Headpiece: diamante tiara; garland of rose-buds; short embroidered veil, batik headscarf; white stetson.

Jewellery: pendant earrings and matching necklace; pearl-studded choker; funky bakelite brooch and bangles.

Lingerie: push-up strapless bra and lace underpants; bustier, garter belt and silk stockings; all-in-one body shaper.

Shoes: petite leather pumps; strappy sequin sandals; white vintage boots; diamante-studded red stilettos.

Handbag: ivory damask shoulder bag; silver lamé drawstring pouch; your great aunt's clutch bag.

your feet so you'll want an extremely comfortable fit. Hours of standing and dancing at the reception will influence you in choosing the most comfortable heel. Another important consideration is your height next to your groom.

You have the choice of buying shoes that are a contrast to your gown or finding a pair that matches the fabric colour of the dress. If the latter proves difficult, some bridal stores will offer to dye the shoes for you at an additional cost.

Handbag

Although a handbag doesn't often come to mind when thinking about wedding accessories, every bride will want a place to put her lipstick, perfume and a tissue or handkerchief. Select a tiny, embellished purse, and assign your chief bridesmaid the task of holding on to it for you once the ceremony is over.

Seasonal considerations

Depending on the time of year, there are a couple of extras to think about.

* During cooler months, you'll want a wrap to keep you warm as you enter and exit the ceremony and reception.

* If there is the possibility of rainy weather, you may want to shop for an umbrella that's large enough to protect you and your dress. Or, perhaps it will be hot, when it might be worth investing in a pretty parasol to provide shade, and a tube of sun cream.

Wedding day beauty

Every bride will want to feel beautiful on her wedding day and it pays to spend some time in advance on how you might achieve this. Natural beauty is the starting point for any good looks and you'll want to play up your physical assets.

Your hair

Consider your options early on so that you have time to try out a couple of styles in the months before the wedding. Do you have a short, face-framing cut that you want to continue wearing or do you want to let it grow out a little for a fluffier effect? If your hair is longer, do you want to wear it up or down on your wedding day? Is your hair colour treated, and if so will it need re-doing in the weeks before the wedding, or do you want something slightly different?

Talk to your hair stylist about your dress and headpiece – take your headpiece to an appointment – so he or she can assess how best to arrange your hair to work with it. More importantly, let him or her determine how to attach the headpiece comfortably so that it stays in place throughout the ceremony and reception.

Make one appointment with your hairdresser to have your hair trimmed and/or colour-treated two to three weeks before the wedding and a second appointment for styling on the day of the wedding. If you are planning something elaborate, make a separate appointment in advance so your stylist can practise creating your wedding day hairdo.

Your make-up

Start a beauty programme at least three months before the wedding. Think about how much of you is going to be on show, and how you want to make the most of it. How can you improve the quality of your skin? Will you need a make-up artist? Do you want to look natural?

Depending on how skilled you are at applying your own makeup, you might be able to do it yourself based on advance consultation with a beautician at your favourite department or speciality store. Tell her about the time and place of your wedding, and describe your gown and headpiece as well as your jewellery. She'll be able to enhance your current make-up application with new shades that are appropriate for the lighting at your wedding. Give yourself plenty of time to practise applying the products yourself.

If you're not particularly expert in putting on make-up, you may want to hire a make-up artist to be sure that your look is perfect from beginning to end. Arrange to have a trial run a couple of weeks before the wedding and decide on the look that suits you the best. Then have the stylist come to your home on the morning of the wedding, at least two hours before you are scheduled to leave.

Focus on you

Face: keep up a daily routine of gentle cleansing, toning and moisturising using top-quality products. Keep your eyebrows in good shape.

Hands and feet: have a monthly manicure and pedicure to keep your nails strong and your skin soft. Apply moisturiser to your hands daily.

Body: exfoliate all over once or twice a week. Moisturise your neck, shoulders, back, legs – and have your legs waxed in the week before the Big Day.

A natural look

An attractive look for a bride on her wedding day is a warm, natural one. Use makeup effectively in order to look your best. Certain products can help erase beauty flaws or flare-ups.

Start with a soft foundation that isn't too white (which can make you appear washed out in the wedding photographs) but which is also consistent with the skin tone of your neck and arms. Complete this first step with finishing powder, applied with a big fan brush.

Even the most well-rested bride will need some under-eye concealer to hide darker tones. Rather than applying a white concealer, place a dab of light concealer in the inner corner of the eye near the bridge and a slightly deeper shade for the outer part of the under eye. Next, choose a shadow in a dusty, natural shade along with liner to define the shape of your eyes, and finish with mascara.

Essential in bringing attention to the eyes is the proper application of blusher, which should only be placed on the cheek to temple area and on the forehead. Blusher should not be applied to the nose or chin.

Your wedding day beauty wouldn't be complete without addressing your fingernails and toenails as well as your skin. Lots of bridal parties join together for an afternoon of manicures and pedicures the day before the wedding. Think about choosing a natural or light pink shade of nail polish.

To tan or not?

On the question of tanning, the decision is yours. A touch of colour can certainly lift your look if you are pale-skinned and wearing white, which may give you extra confidence on the day. Don't overdo it though; a natural look is always best. Don't tan in the back garden; fake tanning options are available in creams and sprays, but try them out with plenty of time to reconsider. Another option is to apply just a dusting of bronze powder on your exposed bits on the day.

Your body

Staying in shape by exercising and eating well will not only help you look gorgeous on the day, but will also offer respite from all the planning, not to mention the occasional tensions that crop up as you try to please a good many people around you.

Shape up

You can immediately look and feel better by adding some physical activity to your daily agenda, and by adopting healthy eating habits. For the maximum benefit, start a new exercise and dietary regimen early on in your planning and not just a couple of weeks before the wedding. You should not be starving yourself at the last minute, in an attempt to drop a few kilos for the Big Day, especially when you will be tired from juggling the final details.

Do not overdo it in the beginning or you may burn out too early. Set up an exercise

What are you eating?

- Never drastically cut back on your food intake hoping to lose weight that way, since your body will rebel and leave you worn down, irritable and exhausted.

- Start the day with a good breakfast. This is the most important meal of the day, and it will kickstart your metabolism, replenish the body's low blood sugar levels and provide you with the energy you need.

- Eat a nutritious snack between major meals to keep your metabolism humming.

- Most meals should include a small portion of lean meat, fish, poultry or pulses.

- Eat at least five helpings of fresh fruits and vegetables a day.

- Sit down for a meal, rather than grabbing food on the run.

- Try to avoid eating dinner very late in the evening.

- Drink plenty of water to keep your complexion clear and your body lubricated.

- Even if you are really determined to drop a few kilos before your wedding day, don't deprive yourself of an occasional treat; just try to make it a healthy one.

schedule that reasonably fits into your busy lifestyle. Talk to your physician or personal trainer to determine what types of exercise would be most beneficial to you and the easiest to fit into your allotted time.

In fact, a visit with your doctor is a great way to start your new routine. Check your weight and blood pressure and have a cholesterol screening. Talk to your doctor about your goals, and ask for a daily calorie count that is appropriate for your height, weight and age.

You'll need a minimum of at least 20 minutes of aerobic activity four to six times a week. Walking, cycling and swimming are activities that you can do alone, and are convenient to fit into any schedule. If you don't have the discipline for lone exercise, a group sport like hockey, netball or tennis might be a better option. Maybe you and your fiancé can even find something that you can do together, which may well be a welcome break from what can easily become constant talk of wedding preparations.

To get the maximum benefit from your exercise programme, integrate some weight training to tone and shape your muscles.

Try both free weights and exercise machines to determine which feels more comfortable to you. In combination with aerobics, weight training helps to build muscle and activate your metabolism. Muscles use up more energy and take up less space than the fat in your body. Just a few weeks of regular exercise can make noticeable improvements to the definition of your arms and legs. (Take note that a bride who diets without exercise will lose muscle tone as well as fat.)

Be sure to let your body rest one day per week and make sure that you are getting plenty of sleep each night and taking the opportunity to relax on the weekends. You should expect to feel a little tired during the first couple of weeks in a new exercise program, but don't push yourself so hard that you are constantly exhausted.

Finally, aim to take in eight to ten glasses of water each day (at least 1.5 litres). This is even more important if you are exercising regularly. If your body tends to retain water, cut back on your sodium intake, which will reduce water retention.

Survival tactics

On a personal level, you will want to look great and feel great on your wedding day. If you are not sure of the impression you want to give, look through a couple of magazines for inspiration, but don't make the mistake of thinking that everything you see will be right for you.

Get it right from the start
It is generally a bad idea to go for a completely new look. Concentrate instead on looking the best version of you, and not someone your guests will barely recognise.

Take a friend
When it comes to buying your wedding gown, sales assistants and bridal consultants will offer you all the professional advice you need, but do not think that it stops there. Take a close relative or friend with you when you shop – someone who knows you well and who can be relied on to be truthful. Picking the right person could be one of the most significant decisions of your entire planning strategy.

Avoid typical mistakes
Whatever you do, don't try anything permanent (like a new hair colour or extensions) the week before your wedding. You need to do this with plenty of time for any misjudgements to grow out.

Similarly, the risks of opening a bottle of nail polish on the Big Day are too great. Instead, invite the girls in your bridal party to come over for an afternoon of manicures and pedicures the day before the wedding.

Emergency slimming aids
If you are finding it impossible to stick to your diet, check out your local salon to see if it offers body-wrap treatments, which include weight-loss, detoxing and body contouring options.

While you are about it, investigate the live-saving world of miracle underwear for a flatter chest or tummy, tighter bum and thinner thighs.

Resources

Finding a dress

Momentos Brides
2 Coneygreen Close
Lower Earley
Reading, RG6 4XE
Tel: 01189 860503
www.momentos-brides.co.uk

Hilary Jane Designs
3 Cheadle Wood
Cheadle Hulme, SK8 6SS
Tel: 0161 4852067
www.hilaryjanedesigns.co.uk

Perfect Day The Wedding Specialist
29 William Street
Lurgan, BT66 6JA
Tel: 028 38 321607
www.perfectdayni.com

Lizanne Bridal & Evening Gowns Ltd
85 Bargates, Christchurch
Dorset BH23 1QQ
Tel: 01202 485958
www.lizannebridal.co.uk

Caroline Castigliano
62 Berners Street
London, W1T 3NN
Tel: 020 7636 8212
www.carolinecastigliano.co.uk

Amber Sorrell Design Couture
2 Maypole Cottages
Elmwood Lane
Barwick-in-Elmet
Leeds, LS15 4JX
Tel: 0113 281 2050
www.ambersorrell.com

Couture

Kuga Couture
Tel: 020 8906 8825
www.kugacouture.com

Elaine Closs
Tel: 020 7801 0821
www.elainecloss.co.uk

Elizabeth Todd
020 7224 2773
www.elizabethtodd.com

On a budget

Déjà Vu Bridal Wear
Tel: 01483 203545
www.dejavubridalwear.co.uk

www.nearlynewbridal.com

www.usedweddingdresses.com

Wedding accessories

www.confetti.co.uk

www.1stcallforweddings.co.uk

Exquisite Bridal Tiaras
Old School House
3 Loughorne Road
Newry, Northern Ireland BT34 ILT
Tel: 028 3026 0566
www.bridaltiara.com

Bridesmaids Direct
32 Roping Road,
Yeovil, BA21 4BD
Tel: 01935 413656
www.bridesmaidsdirect.co.uk

Wedding Garter
Unit 4 Business Centre
John O'Groats,
Caithness, KW1 4YR
www.wedding-garter.com

Kit and Caboodle Ltd
262 Old Farm Avenue
Sidcup, DA15 8AN
Tel: 07990 542 902
www.kitandcaboodle.co.uk

Chapter Six
The Groom's Guide

While you are busy sorting out roses and raffia, or focusing on how to wear your hair, your fiancé should be making a few plans of his own. Not only does he get to arrange your honeymoon, he will also need to organise the men's formalwear, and to work out how to get everyone from A to B on the Big Day. Don't worry if you think the sum of his duties will be too much for him; if he makes the right choice of best man he should get all the help he needs.

Hopes about the honeymoon

Have been reading a lot of celebrity-gossip magazines to get ideas about honeymoons. Wish hadn't. Am sickened that some of them get to enjoy three months in Paris/Rome/New York, whereas J and I will get ten days... Where?

And there's the rub. J is determined to arrange all honeymoon himself. Bless. He is getting more and more manly as months go by. He has even gone suspiciously mysterious about the wedding night. We don't want to stay at same place as the wedding, as guests all staying there and we don't want to face them all the next day. (Is that odd?) Waving to our parents over breakfast – no, thanks. So J has arranged something. Or is planning to. Suppose not vitally important – it's not as if that night will be THE Night. The FIRST night. It'll probably be the 6,000th. Probably be too tired for sex. (Although, I don't know...)

Of course it's traditional for the man to arrange honeymoon, but never thought he'd take it that seriously. This is good, though, as have realised that I'm happy to let him take the lead. I trust his taste and I know that he'll pick us something fab. That's good, isn't it? With some ex-boyfriends, I wouldn't have trusted them to book me a long weekend. But I know J'll see us right.

Have had unexpected bonus too: J's parents have said they'll give us £10,000 as a wedding present. Ker-ching! Obviously, in a sensible world this would be put toward curtains for new house and/or savings account. But, in our world, the real, skint world, a lot will go toward honeymoon.

J has asked me where I'd like to go, as in overseas or home. Visions of Paris/Rome/ New York flashed before my eyes for a brief second, then disappeared – to be replaced by... the Lake District. Yup. I really want to go to the Lake District – partly because I just discovered that both our parents went there on their honeymoons. As they're all still married today, can't help feeling it's lucky. And we get so much more for our money if we don't have to spend such a huge chunk on airfares.

That's all I've been allowed to say, though. He really does want to do it all himself. So he's spending hours on Internet every evening, choosing.

What I'd ideally love is a hotel overlooking Lake Windermere. Did think of self-catering beach house, but don't want to cook. Want to be pampered. Want hotel room service and mini bar. In my vision, we wake up amid rumpled white sheets and look across room to French windows opening out to a lake. There's a knock on the door – breakfast, with snowy napkins and a single red rose. We get up three hours later, stroll to a restaurant for lunch, then go walking in the countryside. Back to hotel, get sexy, have a bath and beautify, then eat dinner on the candlelit verandah, gazing into each other's eyes and telling each other. . .

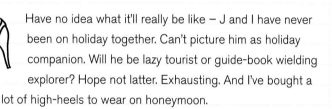

J hasn't really said what he'd like. For once, he's being un-opinionated. He's just asking me lots of questions, and then going all unreadable. Very sexy, that.

Have no idea what it'll really be like – J and I have never been on holiday together. Can't picture him as holiday companion. Will he be lazy tourist or guide-book wielding explorer? Hope not latter. Exhausting. And I've bought a lot of high-heels to wear on honeymoon.

It'll just be nice to be together, after all fuss of planning wedding. Just him and me, with time to remember everything about the day, and plan our future together. Holding hands and gathering sea shells. . .

Oooh! So excited. Really want to ring him up and discuss but – guess what? Engaged. (Like me!) He's on the Internet again.

Back to celeb mags for me. It's all go, this researching. ✳

The basics

Today's grooms are more involved than ever in planning for their special day. There are plenty of tasks that you as a couple can share, but there are also details that your fiancé must complete alone, or at least with the help of his best man.

While some men want to take part in visiting venues and interviewing wedding professionals, helping with the photography, the music or the food, others are less interested in the detail. You should assess your fiancé's level of interest, act accordingly and keep him informed as major arrangements fall into place. However:

✳ It's the groom who selects the formalwear shop and chooses the styles for the men of the wedding party and the fathers. What he wears at the altar is determined by the time and formality of the wedding celebration (see page 93).

✳ Most men take little interest in the bride's or bridesmaids' finery, but the groom should be consulted on the design of the buttonholes.

✳ One job that he must start on early is the plan for the honeymoon, including reservations for the wedding night.

✳ He'll also need to supply addresses for his friends on the invitations list, as well as pitch in writing thank-you notes for gifts from his family and friends.

✳ He will coordinate the transportation details on the wedding day, culminating with the honeymoon getaway.

✳ The groom should play an active role in helping to coordinate the attendants at the rehearsal so that he knows what will take place at each point in the ceremony.

✳ As the wedding day draws closer, he'll need to help with the legal paperwork, choose gifts for his attendants and pick up the wedding rings from the jeweller.

✳ Of course he also needs to take time for his bride throughout the engagement, and try to keep stress to a minimum!

The grand finale

Tradition has the groom taking responsibility for picking the honeymoon destination and making the travel arrangements as a surprise to his new wife, but it's not uncommon today for an engaged couple to make the honeymoon arrangements together.

Once you have an idea of the kind of trip you think you want, it's time to start researching the possibilities. Surf the Internet for images of destinations and attractions, send for information packs from the tourist boards of your favourite holiday spots and consult with a professional travel agent. Determine what your options are, your budget, the time of year you are travelling, and how long you plan to be away.

✱ Do you both enjoy fabulous cuisine and fine dining? Satisfy your cravings with a trip to wine country in the Loire Valley or the Tuscan Hills.

Setting your criteria

- How much time can you spend away?

- Do you want to travel or stay closer to home?

- Do you have a place that is special to you both, or do you want to explore someplace that's brand new?

- Do you prefer the seclusion of a romantic hideaway, or do you want to be caught up in the bustle of a more cosmopolitan setting?

- Do you want warm or cool weather?

- Would choosing an all-inclusive package be easier for you?

✱ Do you want to experience as much as possible in a short period of time? Consider a fortnight's cruise where you can wake up to a new port of call every morning, and be guaranteed plenty of entertainment and activity both on and off the ship.

✱ Are you dreaming of a truly exotic holiday that takes you on an African safari, a trip to the Far East or harbours in the seaports of the Mediterranean Sea? Sign up for a tour, where you really can find the opportunity to be alone as a couple while taking advantage of an experienced guide.

✱ Do you want an athletic experience of sailing your own boat, snorkelling through spectacular reefs, camping on a mountainside or bicycling from one B&B to the next? Do you want to learn how to surf or scuba dive? Investigate the options for a holiday that centres on a sport you both enjoy doing already, or one that you would like to learn.

✱ Or would you prefer to sleep on the beach for the week, soaking up the sun, sipping fruity cocktails and flicking through the pages of glossy magazines?

Hotels and resorts make a business of catering to honeymooners, often with special packages that include unique treats and upgrades. Let the concierge know in advance and you can probably enjoy a few extra perks. Timeshares are another option, with the possibility of trading reservations for anywhere in the world.

Honeymoon travel tips

Don't skimp on the planning for your honeymoon. The last thing you want after the wedding of your dreams is a honeymoon you won't be able to forget for all the wrong reasons. Here are some tips for travelling with ease and not forgetting any of the specifics.

✷ Collect as much material as you can on your chosen destination so that you can take advantage of everything available to you both. Guide books will provide basic information while travel magazines offer more up-to-date activities. Tourist boards will send brochures with points of interest and calendars of special events.

✷ Plan to interview more than one travel agent to find a professional who is really familiar with where you're travelling and can provide expert advice. Some travel agents belong to large corporations that can offer reduced rates on holiday packages. Others may work for independent businesses or for themselves and have certain specialities like adventure tours or exotic getaways.

✷ Knowing that all travel agents are not alike, ask for recommendations from friends who share your tastes in travelling. The best professionals are members of the Association of British Travel Agents. Book an appointment rather than showing up unexpected, and carry a list of questions to discuss during your visit. Double-check the quoted rates with airline and hotel websites, and ask about travel insurance.

✷ Obtain a list of official requirements, and make sure that your personal identification is current. Check your passport and any necessary visas. Inquire about the need for inoculations, and schedule the treatments with your physician in plenty of time before your departure.

✷ Before you book your reservations, coordinate your work schedules to determine how much holiday time you can use, and whether you want to add a day or so afterward to unpack and settle down into married life.

✷ If your leave time is limited, plan a short escape and make plans for a later, longer holiday to your real dream destination when the timing is better. Remember that any private time you have together immediately following the wedding will still be special; an intimate weekend in the country will be just as memorable as two weeks on the ski slopes.

✷ Give some thought as to how you'll get to the departure point and, later, home when you return. Arranging transportation for the newlyweds is one of the duties of the best man, but anyone can take over. You'll want to have your bags packed and ready to go before you head out for the marriage ceremony.

❝❝ My best friend lost her suitcase on holiday and spent three days wearing her husband's clothes. Hoping to avoid the same disaster, I packed a few of my essentials in Jason's case and some of his in mine. Our cases arrived okay, but Jason got an odd look from the official who checked his bags. ❞❞ **Tara, 22**

- Make arrangements for your mail to be handled while you are away. Be sure to leave all your gifts in a safe place, or consider asking a friend to stay at your house in your absence.

- Make copies of your marriage certificate and take one with you. If you have changed your name but have not yet changed your identification documents, travel under your maiden name.

As far as reservations are concerned, you will find it easier to travel under your maiden name until all your documentation reflects your new name. This is especially important in this time of heightened security.

- Pack romantic extras, such as favourite CDs, massage oils and lotions. Of course, don't forget your best lingerie!

Choosing the best man

In the same way that a bride may struggle to choose her chief bridesmaid, a groom often wrestles with the decision about whom he'll ask to serve as best man. The selection of the groom's chief attendant is important for both the symbolism of his role and the duties he'll carry out.

Most often, the best man is the groom's closest brother or cousin, or best friend from school or university. In some cultures, it is traditional for the groom's father to take this honour.

While the best man will receive a list of tasks to fulfill, his main contribution is to support the groom in the decisions he makes, and to be a judge of good taste when it comes to making his speech and arranging the stag night. He needs to be a conscientious listener, to advise the groom throughout the engagement, and to take part in selecting the appropriate formalwear for all the men in the wedding party. His objective is to make the most special day of the groom's life a success.

The relationship between the groom and his best man may well go back further than that of the groom and his bride, and will continue long after the wedding.

What do ushers do?

Typically one usher for every 50 guests will be chosen by the groom and best man to:

● advise guests on the use of flash photography, confetti and mobile phones.

● direct guests to their seats.

● hand out corsages and programmes.

The best man's duties

The best man plays an essential role throughout the engagement and on the wedding day itself, which is focused primarily on activities behind the scenes.

✱ His first active role is typically to assist the groom in picking out the formalwear for the men in the wedding party. In opting for one style over another and offering recommendations for coordinating accessories, he needs to represent the views of the ushers as well as any considerations regarding the bride's outfit.

✱ The best man arranges the stag night. Traditionally this is a night of pub crawling, but more and more commonly nowadays the best man will arrange and host a bloke's weekend away or attendance at a sporting event.

✱The best man attends the wedding rehearsal in order to learn how the ceremony will proceed the next day. It's his job to corral the ushers and to make sure they all know what they are doing and when.

✱ On the wedding day, his most important task is to make sure that the groom arrives at the ceremony on time and fully dressed with all the items of his outfit. The best man carries the wedding rings to the service, and presents them to the clergyman at the appropriate moment.

* Depending on the type of ceremony, the best man will be responsible for delivering the celebrant's payment at a discreet moment.

* At the reception, it's the best man who offers the first toast to the newlyweds. After making his speech he may read out telegrams or e-mails from absent friends, and then passes on to other guests who want to say a few words.

* He makes sure that the bridesmaids have a fleet of dance partners, and double-checks that transportation for the couple's honeymoon getaway is ready on time.

* After the wedding he is often involved in dropping off honeymoon luggage to the hotel the newlyweds are staying in, as well as collecting any rented formalwear for cleaning and return.

“ Being the best man is not a job to take lightly. I was so honoured when Craig asked me to do it that I didn't hestiate to say yes. I wouldn't now, either, but I think I might go about it differently if I got the chance a second time around. I hadn't planned for the overwhelming sense of duty you feel and the terrible fear that if something goes wrong you are letting a real friend down on the biggest day of his life. I have to admit, I didn't enjoy the day itself and only really felt relaxed once the toasts were over. ” **Alex, 26**

The stag night

Admittedly, the bride is the one who is bound to get the majority of attention during the engagement. But when it comes to the stag night, it's time for a guys' night out and all eyes are on the groom.

A best man will typically want to arrange a memorable event for the groom, and one that allows all of the groom's other close mates and family members to demonstrate their support and friendship.

If friends are widely scattered geographically, the stag night needs to be planned with plenty of advance notice to make time for any long-distance travel.

The reputation of the stag night has suffered, provoking most of us to conjure up images of raucous behaviour, heavy drinking and hazardous pranks, that the groom needs weeks to recover from, not to mention causing late arrivals on the Big Day. However, it is more usual for a group of men to want to spend some time together at a fun venue, taking a trip down memory lane and talking of recent adventures.

Often the venue is driven by a sports outing, such as a round of golf or tickets to a rugby match. The event may be preceded or followed by a meal at a favourite restaurant, or a night of clubbing.

Ideally, the stag night should be scheduled way in advance of the wedding, so that there's ample time for any recovery period. Sometimes, the stag and hen nights are hosted simultaneously so the two groups can meet up at a later hour and continue their celebrations together.

Surprise!
An element of the unexpected goes with the territory for a stag night and a groom will need to trust his friends to know what he might or might not enjoy.

Formalwear

When it comes to choosing wedding day attire, the men of the bridal party have a much easier time of it than the women. The appropriate clothes are simply determined by tradition, according to the formality and time of day of the celebration.

t's most important to remember that each usher wears identical attire, which should also be the choice of the fathers and, perhaps, the grandfathers.

What are your options?

* For a formal daytime wedding, choose a classic cutaway coat with grey, pinstripe trousers, grey vest and ascot or four-in-hand tie. Accessories that add a debonair flair are top hat and grey gloves.

* At a formal evening wedding, the groomsmen choose full black dress with a white wing-collar shirt and white piqué vest and bowtie.

* A semi-formal daytime wedding calls for a stroller coat with grey pinstripe trousers, grey vest and ascot or four-in-hand tie.

* The classic tuxedo is proper for a semi-formal evening ceremony. Men can make a choice between a notched collar and shawl collar.

* For a tropical destination wedding, or any celebration taking place in hot weather, a white tuxedo or jacket with black trousers is proper and more comfortable.

* And for the most informal situations, the groom can choose a dark wool suit for autumn and winter, or a lighter linen suit for the spring or summer. Another fashionable choice for summer is navy blazer atop striped or khaki trousers, complete with a straw hat.

This was a second marriage for both of us and we wanted to keep it simple. Lisa chose a plain ivory dress and it seemed fitting for me to opt for a dark brown suit. My best man wore navy. **John, 47**

Survival tactics

Not all grooms will find it easy to settle into the role of organiser when it comes to planning his part of the celebrations, and may well have similar anxieties to the bride when it comes to arrangements for the stag night, and being in the limelight on the Big Day.

The right best man

Most grooms will know who they want to be their best man. If you are struggling over one or two, however, there are several pointers that could help you make a final decision. Firstly, how good are his organisational skills? Secondly, can he be trusted not to embarrass you in his wedding day speech or at the stag night? Don't be forced into making your decision by those around you, and do not think that you must choose a brother, or someone for whom you have previously been best man, over a close friend.

Your wedding style

When it comes to the formalwear, assess the shapes and sizes of the men in your wedding party and be sure to choose an appropriate jacket style; a single-breasted suit can look ill-fitting on a man of stocky stature, while a double-breasted suit can dwarf a taller, thinner man. Consider tying the look in with that of the bride and her bridesmaids by adding a colourful tie or vest, cuff links, cravat or hat. But don't overdo the accessories.

Stag night fears

Don't be fooled into thinking your stag night has to be a secret unless you trust your best man implicitly. He should know you well enough to be able to assess what kind of event you would or would not enjoy, but it does not follow that he will be able to resist the temptation to organise some kind of surprise. Be explicit in your limitations to him if you want to avoid too embarrassing a situation.

The dreaded speeches

There are few people who truly relish the idea of making a speech at a wedding. Although it will be an honour for those you ask, there are aspects of the task that will cause concern. The best advice to them is:

✳ Do not leave writing the speech until the last minute; write down ideas as they come to you throughout the engagement and plan to give them form at least a month before the celebration. You cannot rely on spontaneity to carry you through.

✳ Limit all speeches to a maximum of ten minutes.

✳ Have an agreement with your best man that you will come to each other's rescue in the event of stage fright – it will not happen, but it helps to have the feeling of a safety net.

✳ Keep all speeches clean and avoid referring to issues that will cause embarrassment to other members of the wedding party.

✳ Do not be afraid to practise your speech in front of the mirror in the days before the wedding; the better you know it, the easier it will be to deliver.

✳ For obvious reasons, avoid drinking too much champagne before it is your turn to take the microphone.

Resources

Travel planning

Just Honeymoons Ltd
81b Terrace Road
Walton on Thames, KT12 2SQ
Tel: 01932 230710
www.just-honeymoons.net

Journeys By Design
17 Sussex Square
Brighton, BN2 5AA
Tel: 01273 623790
www.journeysbydesign.co.uk

Cognoscenti
16 Northside Wandsworth Common
London, SW18 2SL
Tel: 0208 874 6146
www.cognoscentiworld.com

GoldenMoments
50 Charter House
Lord Montgomery Way
Portsmouth, PO12SH
Tel: 0800 980 5811
www.goldenmoments.net

The Maldives
The Broadway
Stanmore
Middlesex HA7 4EB
Tel: 020 8515 4844
www.justthemaldives.com

Thailand Direct
020 8515 4815
www.thailanddirect.co.uk

South Pacific Travel
www.island-travel.com

www.venice-weddings.com

All-inclusive honeymoons

Sandals & Beaches Holidays
36 Ives Street
London, SW3 2ND
Tel: 0800 742742
www.sandals.co.uk

Cruises

Carnival Cruise Lines
www.carnival.com

Cruising Holidays
IMH Group Ltd
The Old Mill
Firth Street
Skipton, BD23 2PT
Tel: 01756 693609
www.cruisingholidays.co.uk

Travel advice

Department of Health
www.doh.gov.uk/traveladvice

Formalwear

Formalwear
Waistcoats Direct
32 Roping Road
Yeovil, BA21 4BD
Tel: 01935 413108
www.waistcoatsdirect.co.uk

www.menswear-hire.co.uk

Wedding speeches

Finespeeches.com
89 Hay Green Lane
Bournville, B30 1UP
Tel: 0121 441 2829
www.finespeeches.com

Chapter Seven
Three Months
To Go

If you're feeling scared, anxious or unsettled as the Big Day approaches, try not to panic. This is a huge step you're taking, and it's natural – even expected – to find some doubts creeping in. There are many aspects of getting married that are frightening, but they only get worse if you try to ignore them under a veil of false happiness. This is the chapter for you if your feet are starting to feel just the tiniest bit cold, or if your brain has suddenly started to focus on "What if?"

Pre-wedding doubts

Am so weird. Have been lying awake half night worrying about getting married. Decided to write it down here to get it out and see if it makes sense. I'm so pleased to be marrying J, can't understand why bad thoughts keep creeping in. Not proper bad thoughts either – not ones with any real foundation. Just daft ones like: wives are frumpy. Much sassier just to live with a man, then can leave any minute. Wives are forced to endure all kinds of trauma just for "sake of marriage". Is this true? No. Can still leave, indeed easier with £2,000 diamond ring to pawn for petrol money.

Also worry that J will have second thoughts. Don't expect him to – in fact, he has got nicer since engagement, sweeter and more attentive. Making big effort, flowers etc. (Odd. Thought men relaxed after "getting" you?) But worried that he will start finding reasons to back out. Like, my thighs. Or my love of trashy TV. What was once endearing might become annoying when he realises I'm his forever.

Such a scary word. I mean, I love J and he is only man have ever considered marrying. I want to "buy" him – living together is like renting. I want to (eek) OWN him. He makes me laugh, smile, think. Still surprises me with what he says. And he is sexiest man on planet. But marriage? Forever? Such a long time. See it stretching ahead, with no more dates. Argh! I love dates. I was always good at dating. So no more dates? Ever? Frightening. Bit depressing, too. Know that good couples still make "dates" with each other after marriage, but that seems v. forced. Like "working on the relationship". What does that really mean?

Oh God. It's now 3.00 a.m. and I have to go shoe-shopping tomorrow for wedding boots. If don't get clear head and sleep soon, will break down and cry all over shop assistant. (Which, incidentally, did last week. Saw birthday card with photo of old couple snuggled up on bench by seaside. Lost it totally.)

So, let's get rational. Pros and cons of getting married:

Pros
J all mine
Everyone will know J all mine
Relaxed – no dating anxiety

Living together. Bliss

Get to pamper him without looking like stalker girlfriend

Confirmation of his love for me

Confidence-boosting

Official "couple"

Jewellery

Cons

Wives are frumpy

Sex life will go off?

He has to be with me. Obligation

No freedom. Can't just leave

Can't just book holiday for one (never did, but could want to)

What if fancy men afterward?

No more choice

Decision made

Argh. Feeling no better and now 3.30 a.m. Do I need help? Should I ring J? Not fabulous timing but he should answer and talk to his Future Wife. No, can't ring. Look too odd.

How can you tell if nerves are real, if these are real reasons not to do it, or just cold feet? Jules said when she got married, she had panic attacks. In month before wedding, said she picked fights with Paul all time. Just to get reaction – to test him. Can understand, but not gone that bad yet. (Almost.) Like, want to see how committed he really is. Mum said she thinks J is committed. Dad said he thinks J should be committed, just for thinking about marrying me. Maybe true. Am not sanest girlfriend in world, so he must be keen to consider it. And he bought me this ring. AND he has told all friends and some exes about getting married. AND he EVEN likes me when I have no make-up on and wear his jogging bottoms. So, he likes me when I'm frumpy.

Yes! The perfect man.

Feel better. 'Night. ✳

Deadlines for a countdown

As the months begin to count down, you will be grateful to know which aspects of planning should be completed by this stage and which are major considerations with three months to go.

☐ Send engagement announcements to newspapers, and inform all relatives, both close and distant.

☐ Reserve the venues (the earlier, the better) for the marriage ceremony and the reception and sign all relevant contracts.

☐ Meet with your clergyman to discuss ways to personalise the marriage ceremony and schedule premarital counselling as required by most churches and synagogues.

☐ Consider writing your own vows or choose favourite readings to be included in the service.

☐ Meet with the organist to determine appropriate music for the wedding ceremony and discuss the addition of other musicians or vocalists. Select the music.

☐ Arrange to meet with musical groups who can perform a range of tunes to appeal to the variety of guests at your reception. Enter into a contract that confirms the details.

☐ Invite your family, best friends and close relatives to be members of the bridal party. Discuss their wedding attire and take individual measurements.

☐ Order the bridesmaids' dresses, confirming delivery for at least three weeks before the wedding to ensure adequate time for alterations. If the dresses are made, the orders should be placed six months in advance.

☐ Shop for accessories – shoes and jewellery for the women, ties and vests for the men – to complete their outfits.

☐ Help the mothers and grandmothers to choose their wedding outfits and accessories. Invite the grandfathers to dress in the same style of formalwear as the ushers and fathers.

☐ Deliver final payment on your own wedding gown and headpiece, and schedule two fittings – one as soon as they arrive at the bridal shop and another about two weeks before the wedding.

☐ Make the preliminary menu choices with your caterer, selecting foods best suited for the season and time of day and decide on presentation. Provide a 50 per cent deposit and get a contract that confirms all the details and prices.

" All my friends laughed at me when they saw the complex checklist I had devised for my wedding planning, but I swear it saved me from going mad. I was religious about ticking off tasks as I completed them and it was fantastic to see the 'to do' list shrink as the Big Day approached. It felt like I'd really achieved something. " **Sally, 22**

☐ Schedule appointments to visit with several bakers to review their styles and workmanship. Select one to produce the wedding cake and place the order at least two months before the wedding. Get a receipt for your deposit.

☐ Interview several florists and review portfolios of their work. Identify all your floral needs for the ceremony and reception, bouquets and corsages. Place a deposit for your order as soon as you have set a date for the wedding and confirm your choices.

☐ Review the albums of several photographers to find the best professional for your wedding. Place a deposit to secure the date. If you are going to video the wedding arrange this as well, selecting any music you would like to accompany the scenes, and deciding how much of the wedding day to cover.

☐ Firm up the guest list. Order the invitations, "new home" cards and thank-you notes. Consider hiring a calligrapher to write the addresses.

☐ Tour each of the better hotels near where the wedding will take place to suggest to out-of-town guests. Arrange for a discounted group rate and reserve a block of adjacent rooms if possible.

☐ Arrange limousine service to transport the wedding party and immediate families to the ceremony and reception. Consider a horse-drawn carriage or vintage car for your ride to the reception.

☐ Check on legal requirements for the marriage licence. If you are marrying out of the country, check out the legal requirements and complete any paperwork.

☐ Set up your bridal registry and select wedding gifts and items with your fiancé.

☐ Make reservations for the honeymoon and arrange for immunisations.

☐ Confirm the date and time of the wedding rehearsal with attendants.

Invitations

Allow three months before the wedding to order the invitations and prepare them for mailing. Always order more than you need in the event that you make mistakes or have last-minute add-ons.

Have place cards, response cards, "new home" cards and thank-you notes printed at the same time, adapting your design to suit each. You should not use stationery with your married name until after the wedding, so some brides order a small supply of cards with the initial monogram of their maiden name to send thank-yous for gifts that arrive before the wedding.

Invitation style
The formality of your wedding should dominate your choice of invitations. The most traditional ones are printed on white or ivory paper, are folded on the left like a greeting card, and feature wording just on the top page. Popular variations highlight the wording within a panelled border or include a personal insignia, whilst others are printed on handmade papers or on layered sheets affixed with a bow.

If you are having a super-coordinated theme for your day (see page 26) you will want the invitations to capture the essence of that: bright sunshine colours for a tropical theme, printing on acetate instead of card for a wintry feel, and enclosing tiny sequin hearts for something more glitzy. With the wealth of art materials available – paper that is crinkly at the edges, foil-backed or studded with glitter, and pearly or metallic embossing paints, you can let your imagination run riot.

Once you have chosen the paper style, you'll need to select a font style and whether you prefer engraving or thermography. Formal and semi-formal events typically call for a graceful, flowing script while less formal weddings are better suited to a roman style.

Indeed, if you really want to veer away from tradition, consider sending a wedding invitation in postcard format, or including a novelty gift with the invitation. Just keep in mind that the most important thing is that guests are aware of the details of the wedding and turn up on the right day!

Invitations should be mailed between four and six weeks in advance of the wedding. (Those being sent to another country should be posted at least eight weeks in advance to allow enough time.)

Invitation inserts

The invitation and response cards are placed within an inner envelope addressed with the names only of the recipient. This is inserted into a fully addressed envelope for mailing. Other elements that may also be included:

- "new home" cards: to announce your new address and the date you move in.

- A map with directions to the ceremony and reception.

- Details of overnight accommodation.

- Sequins, pressed flowers, a lottery ticket for a draw on the day.

- A gift list (to be judged at your discretion).

Invitation wording

Since the details of any two weddings are never alike, the wording of invitations varies with each bridal couple and the particulars of their individual wedding celebration. There are no hard and fast rules here, but a few conventions should help you decide what you want. It is usual to identify the hosts of the event – traditionally, the bride's family.

Mr and Mrs Roy Bowling
request the pleasure of the company of

(handwrite guest's name)

at the marriage of their daughter
Madeline Claire to Mr Lucas Duncan
at the Holy Trinity Church
on Saturday, 4th November, 2004
at 3.00 p.m.
Salisbury, Wilts

When the couple is the host of the wedding, or when family ties are extended or complicated, something simpler is called for, as follows:

The honour of your presence
is requested at the marriage of
Miss Amy Michelle Callahan
and
Mr Brian Anthony Evans
on Saturday . . .

If your parents are divorced you have two options. The first is to combine the names of both parents on a single invitation. The second is to send separate invitations to the wedding, one hosted by the bride's mother and the other hosted by the bride's father.

If sending one invitation, the bride's mother's name goes on the first line, whether she has remarried or not. The bride's father's name goes on the second line, without the "and".

Premarital counselling

It's not unusual for couples to hesitate about investing time in premarital counselling on the front end, but when they complete the sessions they often find they have discovered numerous ways to strengthen their partnership.

More and more engaged couples are taking part in premarital counselling in order to build a strong foundation for married life together. In fact, it is not unusual for your clergyman – regardless of your religion – to insist that you and your fiancé attend a series of classes or perhaps a weekend retreat with other engaged couples before the wedding.

What are the benefits?

Participation in such a programme is designed to help each of you understand your individual needs as well as those of the two of you as a couple. Typical subject areas include the way you'll interact with each other after the wedding and improving how you communicate with each other. You'll learn the necessity of balancing time alone and time together, and how to nurture yourself as well as your spouse. In addition to examining the nuances of speaking to each other and your respective families, you'll pay attention to developing better listening habits.

Above all, the sessions will help you gain awareness of the conflict that is inevitable to some degree in any partnership; and that it is perfectly normal for married couples to experience disagreements as they continue to grow together. Based upon your respective childhoods, each of you will have a preconceived idea of the perfect marriage

Marital hot spots

There are a number of issues that can disrupt marital bliss. By discussing them now, there's a good chance you will have some idea how to react to them when they do occur.

Work

Do you intend/need to work once you are married? Don't underestimate a man's pride when it comes to providing for a wife and children, but don't lose sight of your independence either.

Or are you the main breadwinner? In which case how does he feel about becoming a house husband?

Money

If you do not intend to work, how will you and your husband tackle your finances? Will you opt for a joint account or separate ones where he gives you some kind of allowance? If you are both working, how will you decide who pays for what?

Children

Do you both want children? Have you considered what you might do if one or both of you prove infertile? If you intend to keep your maiden name, how will you resolve the names of your children?

Religion/politics

If you differ in faith/opinion, there are bound to be times when it becomes an issue – say one of you is actively involved, or you disagree on the best path for a child. You may have to accept that you will inevitably disagree with each other. Consider seeking impartial advice in such instances.

Sex/infidelity

Your respective sex drives will go through various highs and lows as you age together and this can put a strain on any relationship. What are your views on infidelity? Does he feel the same way? Are there boundaries you can agree on?

Family/friends

You cannot choose your partner's relatives or close friends, many of whom share a history with your fiancé. Learn to spot the good things in people you like less, and find ways to divert your jealousy.

Domestic chores

If you haven't lived together before, you may find the first few weeks of sharing the same home quite difficult. How do you both see the domestic chores divided between you?

and your role within it. You'll learn to "fight fair" in order to avoid the difficulties of "he said, she said", and to analyse what it is that each of you wants from the life ahead of you.

Through this counselling process, couples will recognise their attitudes regarding many of the issues that challenge other married couples and their relationships, such as the handling of money and financial management during the marriage or the various issues surrounding pregnancy, parenting and home life.

No doubt your clergyman will engage in a discussion on the role of religion in marriage and offer his or her assistance in helping the two of you to address conflicts that will arise over the course of years. Religious intermarriage is common today, and couples are taught how their upbringing may affect the priorities in their relationship as well as strategies for having healthy respect for each other's beliefs, whatever they are.

Finally, if either the bride or groom has been married previously, the counselling sessions will help to identify the difficulties in maintaining a happy union and how the two of you can strive to overcome whatever challenges lie ahead.

Family tensions

It's important to remember that a wedding is not just the union of bride and groom, but also the marriage of two families, and this inevitably means a further set of parents and siblings to consider when making your arrangements.

Regardless of how long you have known your future in-laws, there may be tension and anxiety that naturally comes about when planning a wedding which can strain relationships. Those same feelings also hold true within your own family.

Armed with skills in diplomacy and a willingness to accept some compromises, however, engaged couples can help to avoid awkward and stressful encounters by being considerate of everyone's feelings. While traditional wedding etiquette can't solve all the personal conflicts, there are some guidelines that often smooth the stress and strain. Honest communication is the most essential component to keeping peace.

There are a number of situations that might affect you, and it is best to be aware of them from the beginning, so that you can find ways of dealing with them when they come up.

* There are countless brides who don't feel particularly close to their fiancé's sisters and so don't ask them to participate in the wedding party until some emotional eruption reveals their disappointment in not being asked. With a little creativity, you can always find ways to include your fiancé's family in the celebration.

* An overbearing mother or future mother-in-law may want to be closely involved in planning the wedding details. Parents who are financially contributing to the wedding tend to feel that they should have a say. For other parents, the thought of "losing" a child and needing to share them with another family is threatening and gives rise to unexpected behaviour.

* There may be relatives whom you simply don't care to invite. While receiving an invitation to your wedding should be considered an honour, recognise that you may cause ill feelings or perpetuate ongoing family tensions by not including certain people.

* There may be stepparents and stepfamilies whose feelings are more important to you than those of blood relatives, in which case you will have to exercise a certain degree of diplomacy in having them involved.

* There may be other relatives who retain bitterness from a previous family divorce, are reluctant to mingle with the alienated parties and ultimately threaten the joy of the day.

Easing the tension
By anticipating everyone's emotions early in your planning, you should be able to avoid any embarrassing incidents that might tarnish an otherwise perfect day.

You might start out by sharing the classic listing of who does what at a wedding to break the ice and determine their willingness and ability to satisfy the traditional checklist. Try to keep the contributions in line as you will want various expenses to remain in budget. Be tactful when it comes to building the guest list and arranging the reception seating. Make sure that divorced parents

are surrounded with a number of their relatives and friends.

Pay attention to the wording of your invitations, which will be influenced by the relationship between the parents who are hosting the event. Compatible terms can lead to both the mother of the bride and the father of the bride extending the invitation.

Alert the photographer to any potential uneasiness. If you find yourself being photographed in a group that makes you feel a bit uncomfortable, be sure to smile and remember that you're not obliged to purchase every picture.

The father of the bride traditionally escorts his daughter up the aisle, but this could be the responsibility of your brother, uncle, stepfather or closest family friend depending on your circumstances. Wedding etiquette has the mother of the bride the last guest to be seated before the processional, taking her seat of honour in the first pew. If neither parent has remarried, they may agree to sit together.

A stepmother should be seated in the second pew where the bride's father joins her to observe the ceremony. Similarly, the mother of the groom is seated in the first pew, and the father of the groom is seated in the second pew.

If you anticipate any potential awkwardness among any of the immediate wedding party members, avoid the tradition of a receiving line and just make plans to spend more time circulating among your guests after the ceremony.

Think about how to best handle the traditional father–daughter and mother–son dances to be sure no-one is left standing alone on the dance floor.

  I had a real struggle persuading Mum to come to my wedding, even though she and Dad have both had new partners for years. When she finally agreed, I knew I was going to have to be sensitive about seating arrangements, but did not want to feel totally beholden to her. I decided we would sit with her and Bob for the first two courses of the meal, and then to swap seats with my chief bridesmaid and her boyfriend so that we sat with Dad and Nancy for the rest of the meal and the toasts. **Daisy, 34**

Survival tactics

Feelings of pressure and frustration are widespread among women trying to juggle a personal life, a professional life and planning a wedding. Instead of the picture-perfect engagement, you may well experience tears and tension as you work to meet deadlines and keep everyone smiling.

While there will be stressful moments as all eyes are upon you and everyone has a view about the Big Day:

* Don't be surprised if your fiancé is having a similar experience. The secret to keeping everything from spinning out of control is communication, honest and often, between the two of you and your families. Use your imagination and your creativity to deal with resolving any conflict.

* Remember your priorities: at any given stage of the planning process you will feel that there are a hundred and one details to take care of. Keep current lists of the tasks at hand and tackle the most important things first, one at a time to keep from becoming flustered.

* If you find it impossible to juggle everything from day to day, establish a fixed routine. Set aside an hour at the same time every day just to work on your wedding plans.

* Get some help: some of the best advice is to try delegating tasks to the bridesmaids and family members who want to help. Your inner circle will become even closer in the process, and you'll be positively relieved to get some of the responsibilities off your plate.

* Have a deadline: make sure that the planning is over at least a week before your wedding, and slow down your activities as the Big Day approaches.

* Get some sleep: be sensible about what you can achieve in one day and go to bed at a reasonable hour. Sleep as late as you like on the day of the wedding, while allowing ample time to pamper yourself as you dress.

* Keep it simple: with so many details to manage, you'll want to impose some simplicity to help the work remain within reach. It's obvious that by reducing the time-consuming and pointless irritations, the planning will proceed with less effort for everyone involved.

* Look after yourself: it's important not to forget good nutrition and rest every day. Your metabolism needs to be in top condition for you to function properly, so make sure you eat a balanced diet and drink plenty of water, especially if you are exercising regularly.

* Take a break: if it all gets too much, take some time out to plan a quick weekend getaway for you and your fiancé. You'll come back feeling refreshed and ready to take up the reins again.

* Stay positive: remember that there is an end in sight to all the preparations you have been making, and nothing need stop you getting there (eventually).

Resources

Premarital counselling

Relate
Herbert Gray College
Little Church Street
Rugby, CV21 3AP
Tel: 0845 130 4010
www.relate.org.uk

Marriage care (formerly the Catholic
 Marriage Advisory Council (CMAC))
1 Blythe Mews
Blythe Road
London, W14 0NW
Tel: 020 7371 1341
www.marriagecare.org.uk

Accord N.I.
N.I. Regional Office
Cana House
56 Lisburn Road
Belfast, BT9 6AF
Tel: 028 9023 3002
www.accordni.co.uk

The Association of Inter-Church Families
35-41 Lower Marsh
London, SE1 7RL
www.aifw.org
Advice to couples from different Christian
 denominations.

The Council of Christians and Jews
1 Dennington Park Road
West End Lane
London, NW6 1AX
Tel: 020 7794 8178
www.accj.org.uk

Stationery

Amore
11 Sandy Vale
Haywards Heath, RH16 4JH
Tel: 01444 473 388
www.amoreweddings.co.uk

Table Plans by Design
Spiral House
Buxworth, SK23 7NL
Tel: 01663 734730
www.tableplans.co.uk

Transportation

Nottingham Horse and Carriage Company
327 Leake Road
Ridgeway, Gotham
Nottingham NG11 0LE
Tel: 01159 831659
www.nottingham-horse-and-
 carriage.company.co.uk

Scottish Wedding Consultants
13 Roman Court
Pathhead,
Midlothian EH37 5AH
Tel: 01875 320490
www.scottishweddingconsultants.co.uk

Wedding Daze Ltd
250 Ashley Road
Parkstone
Poole
Tel: 01202 710850
www.weddingdaze.co.uk

www.1stcallforweddings.co.uk

www.wedding-service.co.uk

Chapter Eight
Two Months
To Go

With just eight or so weeks to go, it must be coming up to the hen night. How do you plan the perfect party – or how do you have your bridesmaids plan it for you? Should it be a lingerie party? A day at a spa? A meal at your favourite restaurant where you reminisce about the past and speculate about the future for Mrs. . . or is it going to be Ms? Are you going to change your name? Do you want to? What does your fiancé think? Don't worry about a thing – this chapter has it all, plus a list of everything you need to get done this month to keep your wedding on track.

Expectations for the hen night

Have moral dilemma. How can I word the hen night invitations without sounding like I'm basically saying, "please come to my house and buy me presents?" Of course that IS what I'm saying... And everyone'll know... But still...

Really want a wild night out with the girls. Thinking back to some of the hen nights I've attended, the greatest have been when we all go away for a whole weekend. Jules's was awesome – we hired a luxury boat and went sailing off the coast. We didn't have to do anything on the boat, except lie on the deck sipping gin and tonics. Heaven. That's what I'd love. It was expensive though – and everyone I know is broke.

Other ideas: weekend in Ibiza? Dancing, nightclubs, me dressed up in big white fake veil – no. Weekend at health spa: beauty treatments, manicures, leg waxing, bikini waxing, spots breaking out, facial allergic reactions, looking like burns' victim on wedding day – no. Quite civilised dinner near home, back by 11pm, no dancing, just mature conversation – no.

Argh! What can I do? Could have a party at my flat... Maybe... But lot of hassle just before wedding. Plus have to move out of here in next couple of months and a party will mean more cleaning. Anita is keen to arrange something, but it's all being held up by my not knowing what I want. She says she'd prefer a quiet evening, if it were her hen night. But she's more of a homebody than me. I want a riotous time. Hmm.

Talking to J earlier about his stag night. His best man has arranged it, and it's a day of hunting/shooting/fishing, then some go-kart racing, then a dinner. There'll be about seven of them. Sounds good.

This is stupid but... I do want to have as good a time as he does. I don't want to be doing something yawnsome if HE'S going to be out going mad. Don't think he'll have strippers, but never know. Don't trust his best man at ALL. Anything could happen.

Sorted. Anita has booked a weekend in Brighton! Six of us: me & A, Emma, Jules, Liz and Ed (counts as woman cos he's gay). We're staying in a pretty hip hotel (top-of-the-range for the bride-to-be) and they have offered a deal because it's out of season. There are several nightclubs and loads of bars. So we can have everything: drinking, dancing and (let's hope) some fun. Plus Liz is going to bring loads of beauty stuff to give us all treatments, and Ed has learned how to read fortunes with playing cards.

Of course, I will not kiss anyone. I don't mean the girls or Ed. I mean strangers. On TV last night was drama about woman who met ex-boyfriend while out partying week before her wedding, and dumped fiancé within three hours. All v. exciting and passionate, but unlikely for me. For one thing, only men likely to meet on my hen night are yobs. Mmmmmm. Hold me back!

Writing this after no sleep for three days. Ugh. Not drinking again till wedding, if ever. What happened to quiet weekend Anita promised me? Ed is in state of shock – said he never knew girls were so predatory and he's glad he's gay.

Went out Sat night to beach bar. Was quiet and we would have gone home had not a local football team arrived. They were all drunk and said we all looked gorgeous! They knew of a party, and after 0.4 seconds' contemplation, we decided to join them. Was in nearby house – quite studenty. But loads of booze. I mean LOADS. The bath was full of ice and beer. (Woke up next A.M. with bottle of vodka down bra.)

Had relatively quiet time personally, but Ems, Liz and Ed got v. drunk. Ems ended up kissing football captain under tarpaulin-covered boat in front drive. Liz almost got in fight with other player's girlfriend and Ed was scared of the house dog, so cowered in the kitchen.

Got back to hotel at seven to find the keys in room door and Liz asleep on sofa!

Ugh. J asked me for details and I lied a bit. Said was v. quiet, lets-try-new-hairstyles sort of thing. Partly hate that it sounds so dull, but mainly long for peace and quiet and a month's sleep. Hope will recover before Big Day. Eek – gotta go. . . Eugh. . . ✳

Deadlines for the countdown

This is where your planning skills really come to the fore. You should be well on the way to finalising most of the critical aspects of the day, and remember – an ounce of organisation now is worth a pound of panic on the day.

☐ Create your own system or spreadsheet for the guest list, invitations, gifts received and thank-you notes written.

☐ Address the envelopes for invitations and insert each of the items. Sticker the postage on each outer envelope and response envelope. Mail the invitations six weeks before the wedding.

☐ Design a wedding programme that describes each part of the ceremony and names the members of your wedding party.

☐ Double-check that the celebrant, bridesmaids, ushers and all others involved in the ceremony are available and know when to attend the wedding rehearsal.

☐ Pick out the wedding bands and specify any desired engraving for each ring.

☐ Make one appointment with your hairdresser to have your hair trimmed two to three weeks before the wedding and an appointment on the Big Day.

☐ Assess the need for babysitting services or special activities for the young children of your bridal party members and guests.

☐ Invite close relatives and special friends not in the wedding party to perform honoured tasks on the day, including presiding over the guest book, pouring champagne or helping to cut and serve the wedding cake.

☐ Purchase special gifts for each member of the wedding party. Look for items that can be personalised with names and the date of the celebrations.

☐ Find a service to preserve your wedding bouquet, and request a pretty "toss bouquet" from your florist to toss when you leave the reception.

☐ Purchase any accessories, such as the ring-bearer's pillow, a guest book, toasting goblets and cake knife.

☐ Schedule a tasting of the wedding meal for about six weeks before the wedding so that there is enough time to make minor changes.

☐ Schedule a tasting with your cake baker to decide on the cake and icing flavours, and design the top tier to preserve.

☐ Check there will be reserved parking spaces outside the ceremony site for autos transporting the wedding party, and obtain necessary parking permits.

☐ Shop for your going-away outfit and clothes to wear on honeymoon. Buy new luggage if you need it.

☐ Schedule physical examinations for each of you and arrange for any immunisations required for your honeymoon travel plans.

What's in a name?

As your wedding approaches, you will need to decide whether or not to change your surname. You are not legally obliged to do so and there are pros and cons with both options.

Until the 1970s, it was a common tradition for brides to take their new husband's last name as their surname. Today, however, more and more brides are giving significant thought to the choices they have in selecting a name that they'll use for the rest of their life.

What are your options?
✽ You can change your maiden name to your husband's surname. It is traditional, and it may be his preferred choice.

✽ You can keep your maiden name as a middle name, perhaps hyphenated with your husband's. (Your husband may wish to use this new name as well.)

✽ You can opt to keep your maiden name, or to use it for your professional life, while taking your husband's surname for all other situations.

✽ Your husband can take your maiden name as his surname.

Things to consider
✽ If you have established a professional identity changing your name may cause confusion or be unwise.

✽ If you are the last descendant to carry the family name, you might feel it is a shame to lose it.

✽ Will your groom support your choice? Is he open to the idea of changing his name?

✽ Will your decision work for the future, especially if you have children?

What are the practicalities?
While taking your husband's name by signing the marriage licence is a legal requirement, you must still change your name on all of your personal and business records as well. On return from your honeymoon, contact Department of Social Security, your motor licensing bureau, your bank, accountant and any other professional with whom you do business.

Showers and hen nights

A bridal shower is an American custom growing in popularity in the UK. Friends of the engaged woman "shower" her with gifts and openly indulge her with lots of attention. Like a hen night, it is an exclusively "girlie" affair and held during the planning period.

Shower etiquette

Invitations to a shower should be mailed about four weeks in advance of the party, and usually friends and distant relatives host the event. (It is considered in poor taste for members of your immediate family to entertain a gift-giving gathering where you carry off a raft of offerings.) Furthermore, two showers or more are considered greedy, although it is possible to bend this rule when the guests at each get-together are a different crowd. Friends at work, family friends and social friends might be invited to separate occasions.

For the most part, this is your chance to spend time with close girlfriends, reminiscing about past times together. Showers are primarily characterised by a theme, and are usually organised around afternoon tea or evenings at home. Sometimes bridal showers are themed around a particular group of gifts. For example, the hostess may choose an area of your first home to furnish, like the kitchen, and guests will supply the everyday dinnerware and table linens, cookware,

appliances and gadgets. Another popular idea is a lingerie shower, where guests are required to bring only lovely items of underwear for the bride (and groom) to enjoy on the honeymoon.

Stag nights and hen nights

Stag nights and hen nights are parties to celebrate the passage from singlehood to marriage, just before the Big Day. These parties can range from the extreme to the quite tame, depending upon the personalities of the bride and groom.

Popular choices for the hen's party are to have a night out over dinner in a favourite restaurant, for instead day at the beach or a spa weekend. Also popular is a night of pub-crawling and dancing that doesn't leave everyone exhausted the next day.

A hen night can also have a theme that is supported with a costume for the bride and activities for each of the attendees to participate in.

Shower fun

- Brides traditionally slide the giftwrap ribbons from each giftbox, since a broken ribbon is said to be unlucky.

- The chief bridesmaid scoops up the ribbons and bows to fashion a novel bouquet for the bride to carry at the wedding rehearsal.

" My fiancé wanted to keep our honeymoon a secret but I was cross because I needed some idea about what to pack. So he got together with my chief bridesmaid and all the gifts at my shower were for the honeymoon. They gave me sun cream, a snorkel and flippers! I didn't know the exact destination, but I had a good idea of the kind of holiday I was getting. It was a great idea! " **Charlie, 37**

Gifts for the attendants

Many brides and grooms buy gifts for their attendants. Traditionally, they are presented to the recipients at the wedding rehearsal, on the morning of the wedding, or when the speeches are made during the reception.

Some brides and grooms choose an identical item for each attendant, while others choose a personal gift for each bridesmaid and usher. An automatic gift for each attendant might be an accessory to complete his or her wedding day attire (in which case they should receive it at least by the morning of the wedding).

For bridesmaids, a jewellery set with matching necklace and earrings is a popular choice, while for the ushers a dapper silk vest to slip on under a tuxedo or handsome cufflinks are both suitable options. Perhaps the gift can also be personalised with the date of the wedding or the recipient's initials.

Depending on the type of wedding you have, the involvement of the attendants, or the spirit of the day, there is no limit to the choices you may make for gifts.

For the girls

* Traditional: jewellery box, picture frame, compact or hand mirror, crystal or silver bud vase, engraved letter opener.

* Personal: her favourite perfume, a personalised journal, bracelet or charm, a favourite book, invitation to champagne and oyster soirée.

For the boys

* Traditional: pen and pencil, pocketknife, grooming kit, desk clock, sports watch.

* Personal: silk tie, monogrammed handkerchiefs, cologne, box of hand-rolled Cuban cigars.

"When Charlie and Amanda got married we knew they were bound to do something different. They had a movie theme and each guest came as his or her favourite character from a film. The happy couple dressed up as John Travolta and Uma Thurman in *Pulp Fiction*. They looked amazing. When it came to the gifts for the attendants, all the boys got pump-action water pistols and the girls had little black wigs and scarlet lipstick. We had a ball at the reception." **Trish, 34**

Survival tactics

A hen night or shower can present a whole host of awkward situations and embarrassments. Whatever you are planning, it pays to bear a couple of typical pitfalls in mind.

✱ It is likely that your bridesmaids will be included as guests at every event in your honour, and this could turn into a financial burden for them. If you want to avoid potential animosity, discreetly mention that you look forward to them joining in the festivities and request that they not feel obliged to bring gifts.

✱ For many brides-to-be the hen night turns into an unpleasant memory if too much alcohol or wild activity is a mainstay of the event. Make sure you choose the right person to arrange your party, someone you can rely on not to resort to cheap gimmicks or shock tactics on the night.

✱ Whether or not you are party to the adventure planned for your groom, don't waste time or energy worrying how his evening might be going. Leave your fears at home and make the most of your own rite of passage.

✱ Amid the thank-you letters that follow your engagement and the ones for wedding gifts that arrive before the Big Day, it is easy to forget to thank people for the shower party and gifts. Ask the hostess to keep track of each gift and giver and present you with a final list.

Resources

Hen parties

www.blackpoolhenparties.co.uk

Weekends by design
Tel: 0870 321 9600
www.nights-weekends.co.uk

Freedom Ltd
Ability House
121 Brooker Road
Waltham Abbey, EN9 1JH
Tel: 0870 787 5959

Cocky Hen
www.cocky-hen.com

Red Seven Leisure
Tel: 0870 751 7377
www.redsevenleisure.co.uk

Call of the Wild Adventure Activities
6 Commercial Street,
Seven Sisters
Neath, SA10 9DW
Tel: 01639 700388
www.callofthewild.co.uk

Changing your name

UK Deed Poll Service
Tel: 0800 7833048
www.ukdps.co.uk

UK Passport Service
Tel: 0870 521 0410
www.ukpa.gov.uk

Change Your Name
Freepost
Orpington, BR6 6BR
Tel: 01689 853645
www.changeyourname.co.uk

Gift list

Marks & Spencer Gift List
Tel: 0845 603 1603
www.marksandspencer.com

John Lewis Gift List
Tel: 020 7828 1000
www.johnlewisgiftlist.com

The Fairy Godmother
44a Ashingdon Road
Rochford, SS4 1RD
Tel: 01702 531194
www.thefairygodmother.co.uk

Bliss Gift Consultancy
32A High Street
Norton
Stockton on Tees, TS20 1DN
Tel: 01642 648744
www.blissgiftconsultancy.co.uk

Rainbows (Master Craft Affiliated)
Earlswood Lakes Craft Centre
Wood Lane
Solihull, B94 5JH
Tel: 01564 700008

Chapter Nine
One Month To Go

Can you believe it? In less than a month it'll all be over.
You've come so far that you might be tempted to relax and
kick back this month. Don't be fooled. There's still a list of
chores for you to do. But don't worry – getting busy is the
best way to keep last-minute nerves at bay. In addition to
the deadlines for this month, you'll find advice on the odd
contingency plan for when (if) something goes wrong.

The rehearsal

Well, THAT was calming! There's nothing like a wedding rehearsal to get you going. Going off the deep end, that is. Just got back, and J is here too, being an angel and making me night cap. (Aaah.) But anyway, the rehearsal. It was so funny.

We all turned up at the vineyard this afternoon, just after lunch. Mum and Dad were beaming and really excited. Anita and Joe were both worried about what they had to do when and if they'd fall over/giggle/accidentally marry each other. J was calm as anything, and I was stressed because my pre-wedding haircut had gone wrong. My fringe is SO short. I look like I've grown an extra 3 cm of forehead… So not my wedding vision. Couldn't concentrate on anything, until they all went into the stables and Dad, Anita and I were left outside.

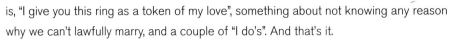

Got bit tearful. When the music started and the waiter opened the door, all I could see was J standing at the end of the room waiting for me. Brilliant! Just wanted to run up to him (hmm, will I ever learn to play it cool?) but Dad insisted we did the proper wedding march – slowly. Sloooowly. So slowly that I got the giggles, which set Mum off too. Dad got a little grumpy then.

The celebrant went over the vows really quickly, and I was quite relieved that I didn't have much to say. It's not like a church wedding: the vows are very brief. All we say is, "I give you this ring as a token of my love", something about not knowing any reason why we can't lawfully marry, and a couple of "I do's". And that's it.

Nick read out the poem we're having and deliberately messed it up for laughs. He's threatening to cough during that bit of the service where the celebrant asks if anyone knows a reason why we can't marry. A tiny part of me sort of hopes that an ex will appear and stand in the aisle, screaming, "Kaaaaaate!" (like in *The Graduate*), but I don't know anyone who's that keen. Even R, who felt "physically sick" a couple of months ago, is now dating someone else. Schmuck. Why don't men carry torches any more? Am I so easy to get over?

J got mushy after the rehearsal and said that it was really starting to sink in now. What? He's cutting it a bit fine! But I know what he means. Up until now it's been a bit like a dream, or planning a party. Going through it today has really made it "real". Asked him if he was having second thoughts and he was brilliant – he said he'd never had a moment's doubt from the day we met. . . just months and months of them. Which was almost the loveliest thing anyone's ever said to me. Almost.

All went out to dinner afterwards. J's Mum booked massive table at fab Italian restaurant. Not just the wedding party, but a ton of J's relatives too – all staying nearby, so quite a crowd. Really loved it, such a relief after stress of the rehearsal. Mum and Dad seemed to kick back a bit too – joking around with Nick and Anita. All having such a good time that no one minded me and J leaving before dessert. Just wanted to get back to mine for some quiet time together (his idea, not mine, wonder what he has in mind. . .).

Actually, still have loads to do. I've been packing up my stuff to move out. That brings it home. I've had such a good time in my single-girl pad. Dinner parties, dates, sleepover parties. . . When I think of leaving, I get a bit upset. Had such a lovely time here. And this is the flat where J and I had our first kiss, out in the hallway. That still makes me tingle to think of it. This is where he first tried to wrestle my top off me on our second date, to no avail. This is where I played hard to get on the third – and where I eventually gave in, on the sixth. I've cooked him dinner here (and burnt it), I've served him cocktails (and spilt them), and I've even made him a birthday cake (got the number of candles wrong!). It's the apartment he's arrived at so many times, carrying flowers and champagne and presents. . . It's also where he told me he loved me. Sniff!

Got to stop thinking like that or I'll never leave. Must go and see if J needs any help in the kitchen, and if his top needs wrestling off. . . ✳

Deadlines for the countdown

If anything is likely to go wrong, it will be in the last few weeks before the wedding. In addition to taking care of the finishing touches for the day – sorting out your beauty arrangements, choosing a gift for your fiancé – make sure you keep close tabs on all the pros.

☐ Set up a meeting at your church or synagogue to determine the logistical procedures for your wedding day, including where you and the wedding party can dress before the ceremony, where the flowers should be delivered.

☐ Order a white aisle runner for the processional to add a touch of elegance and protect the train of your gown from becoming soiled.

☐ Revisit the wedding sites with your photographer and videographer, and review your picture list.

☐ Consult with the band director for your reception to select the bridal waltz as well as the rest of the reception music.

☐ Ask your caterer to pack a picnic basket for you and your husband to take when you leave the reception.

☐ Double-check the reception site's policy on tossing flower petals as the two of you leave for the honeymoon.

☐ Consult a make-up artist about your wedding day look and test new cosmetics well in advance.

☐ Schedule an appointment a few days before the wedding for a full manicure and pedicure.

☐ Select a hospitality gift that can be delivered to the hotel room of each out-of-town guest, including maps of the area, and directions to the wedding and reception venues.

☐ Keep up with writing thank-you notes for the multitude of gifts and well wishes that arrive at this time.

☐ Spend a pampering day at the beauty salon with your bridesmaids, enjoying massages, manicures and pedicures. Encourage your fiancé to enjoy a similar day with his groomsmen, perhaps with a round of golf and relaxation treatments.

☐ Purchase a supply of umbrellas if the weather forecast suggests there will be rain on your wedding day. Choose a particularly pretty one for yourself.

☐ Confirm the honeymoon travel arrangements and collect passports, visas and traveller's cheques for the trip. Assemble receipts for the airline tickets, car rental, hotel reservations and any excursion packages.

☐ Choose a personal gift for your groom that can be presented during a private moment alone together.

☐ Make a list of the bills that will be due on the Big Day, and add appropriate tips for the people who will serve you.

☐ Open joint bank accounts and determine who will be responsible for looking after them and paying the bills.

☐ Check with your home contents' insurance to confirm that your wedding gifts are going to be adequately protected, and review your joint insurance policies to take account of your new circumstances.

☐ Notify each of your employers and/or your insurance agent(s) of your upcoming wedding day and the need to name your new spouse as the beneficiary of any life insurance policy.

☐ Consult with a solicitor to name each other the beneficiaries in your wills.

☐ Complete all the necessary documents to change your name.

☐ Decide upon the favours to be given to each guest at the reception.

The wedding rehearsal

Typically, in the week leading up to the wedding – even on the last day – all of the attendants and immediate family members will meet with the officiant for a run through the ceremony. Under the watchful eye of your wedding director, everyone will learn where he or she is supposed to stand and when he or she is supposed to move.

This is a great opportunity for you to see the wedding as an onlooker. As the bride, your best vantage point may be in the back of the sanctuary observing the ritual unfold as your guests will on the day. Do you approve of the placement of the members of the wedding party? Do you approve of the pace of the processional and recessional? Is the volume of the music at a pleasing pitch?

Take whatever time is necessary for everyone to practise the ceremony process, and if there are children in the wedding party, try to keep them focused.

It's also vitally important for you to have the opportunity of stepping up the aisle on your father's arm and walking to the beat of the music. Don't forget to practise handing over your bouquet to your chief bridesmaid when you reach the altar. At the end of the mock wedding, take back your flowers, reach for your groom's arm or clasp hands and practise taking your first steps as newlyweds.

This may be the first time many of the people involved in different aspects of your wedding come together so it can be a perfect opportunity to arrange a meal after the rehearsal. Keep it informal, and consider holding it at a restaurant close to the rehearsal site, in order to make it as easy as possible for the attendants and family to make it.

Be sure to introduce everyone – especially those ushers and bridesmaids that will be matched for the recessional.

It might help to think through before the rehearsal the pairing up of the bridesmaids and ushers, rather than bumbling through this during the rehearsal. Think about which attendants will get on well with each other and avoid pairing a couple that may look mis-matched when they are walking together.

Contingencies

Let's face it. At some point in the planning of your wedding, something is bound to go wrong. By recognising this possibility in advance and making plans for some swift alternatives, you can avert disaster and no-one need know of the potential calamity.

As the wedding day approaches
You've been up to your ears in planning the wedding for months now, so you're in the best position to quickly shift gears and deal with any situation that arises.

First and foremost it is essential you stay in regular contact with the professionals who are providing services for the day. Even the top professionals can experience a blunder in their business, but should also have contingency plans of their own.

Although disruption to most aspects of the wedding will be tedious – the florist cannot supply the flowers you have specified, the baker has misinterpreted your brief, the photographer has double-booked – there is very little that cannot be remedied. Only you know what you were expecting and your guests will certainly not be aware of any last-minute alterations.

When it comes to what you and your wedding party are wearing, however, it can take strength of character to overcome a disaster. If you find that nerves and excitement are combining to cause you to lose weight, schedule another fitting of your gown about a week before the wedding. Be prepared to pay for the rapid turnaround service, but be thankful to know that your gown will fit you perfectly when it matters.

Stay on top of the delivery of the bridesmaids' gowns. If you get the feeling that the gowns won't arrive in time for the wedding, ask the boutique to help identify a quick-ship supplier who can replace the original order or check the selection at a nearby department store where you can buy dresses off the rack.

Formalwear speciality stores are usually staffed on the weekends to take care of any last-minute tailoring. Be sure that all of the men of the wedding party try on their rented formalwear early enough to address any poor fits.

On the day of your wedding
For peace of mind on the Big Day, it might be a good idea to entrust a close friend to visit the ceremony and reception sites to be sure that the flowers have arrived, the catering stations have been arranged, and the cake is set up where it should be. They can also make confirming telephone calls to the limousine service, musicians, photographer and videographer.

If one member of the wedding party falls ill, you have the choice of replacing them with someone with a body shape that can slip into the chosen attire (this can be as easy as it sounds) or simply rearranging the line-up to accommodate the absence.

" I had got so wrapped up in the planning that I was obsessed with every tiny detail. One of the bridesmaid's dresses came with a fault in the embroidery and I completely lost it. I think all the nervous energy building up finally came out in one huge outburst. It was probably quite good for me, thinking about it, but I made a real fool of myself. " **Stephanie, 28**

Survival tactics

If you find it difficult to imagine keeping calm in the face of pending disaster, just remind yourself of the complexity of your planning process and congratulate yourself on getting so much *right*. If that doesn't help, there are others ways of pulling through.

* Rest assured that you will know at an early stage whether one supplier or another is going to be reliable or not. Trust your instinct on this and be firm in your instruction.

* If you have serious concerns about getting what you want from a professional, find someone else. You cannot afford to give anyone the benefit of the doubt.

* When you are looking for suppliers first time round, keep the contact details of all your second choices, and put them somewhere that is easy to find. In most cases it will be a simple phone call that saves the day.

* Don't rely on suppliers to keep you informed. Double-check their deadlines and make sure they come through. As a rule, do not let anything slip by more than five days. If they do, have no shame in chasing them relentlessly.

* Remember you are not alone in this, particularly as the day gets nearer. If something goes wrong, call up your fiancé, your Mum or a bridesmaid for support. A problem shared. . .

* Once you get to the day before the wedding, make final confirmations and similar jobs someone else's responsibility. Chances are you won't even know about the odd eleventh-hour dilemma, which is how it should be.

* If a supplier really lets you down on the day, remain calm, take it in your stride and do not let it spoil your wedding. You can take it up with them when you get back from your honeymoon.

Resources

Insurance

Weddingplan
1 Prince of Wales Road
Norwich, NR1 1AW
Tel: 08707 744065
www.weddingplaninsurance.com

Allianz Cornhill Wedding Insurance
Jackson Emms & Co Ltd
Oxford House
Reading, RG1 7UZ
Tel: 0118 957 5491
www.weddingsurance.co.uk

Event Insurance Services Ltd
Event House
20A Headlands Business Park
Ringwood, BH24 3PB
Tel: 01425 470360
www.events-insurance.co.uk

Confetti and alternatives

Carnmeal Cottage
Carnmeal Downs
Breage, Helston, TR13 9NL
Tel: 01326 522901
www.bridal-sundries.co.uk

Partybox Ltd
17 Wintonlea
Monument Way West
Woking, GU21 5EN
Tel: 01483 755346
www.partybox.co.uk

Talking Tables Ltd
35 Foxbourne Road
london SW17 8EN
Tel: 020 8767 6000
www.talkingtables.co.uk

Dancing

Mr. Wonderful Dancing
89 Knights Manor Way
Dartford, DA1 5SB
Tel: 01322 290751
www.mrwonderfuldancing.com

UK250 Limited
2 Alpha House
Farmer Ward Road
Kenilworth, CV8 2ED
Tel: 01926 863004
www.uk250.co.uk

Avoiding disaster

www.userbride.com

www.weddingmag.com

http://weddings.about.com

Chapter Ten
One Week To Go

Everything is arranged and all there is time for now is a last-minute panic. Fancy that? Of course not! So here's how to keep cooler than the cucumber in the icebox. We have everything you need to allay your fears, from long, hot herbal baths for beating stress to mantras you can repeat as you sail up the aisle. You'll find your final checklists for deadlines here, as well as a wedding day timetable to keep things on track.

Pre-wedding tremors

So this is it. I'm getting married tomorrow. From tomorrow, I'll be married. I'll be a Mrs. No more Miss. I'll officially belong to someone. I'll be betrothed. I'll be able to tell old wives' tales ('cos I'll be an old wife). I'll have a husband. I'll be able to tell plumbers and car mechanics, "You'll have to deal with my husband". I'll have a wedding ring that'll stop me ever being chatted up again – bah. But I'll be able to have sex whenever I like – yay. I'm really excited. I'm really scared. I'm absolutely, positively sure I'm doing the right thing, but I don't really know.

Absolutely everything is arranged now. My dress is hanging up on the cupboard at the foot of my bed – Mum put it there so it's the first thing I see when I wake up (cheesey, but I like it). I've spent today in the little beauty salon round the corner, having my nails painted and eyebrows shaped. (Should have done that years ago – it looks fab.) All the hen night girls came, even Ed, though we had to stop him having Botox injections in his lips. My legs are shaved, my fake-tan has developed, my makeup is laid out on the dressing table. Anita and Becky are downstairs with Mum, Dad and Nick, and my honeymoon suitcase is packed and ready to go beside my bed.

How do I feel? Weirdly calm... With bouts of hysteria. Can't stop smiling, and waves of happiness, joy and delight keep taking me by surprise at the oddest moments. I'm pleased to be getting married, actually doing it – it feels like I've been "chosen". I don't have to be a singleton any more, a one-woman band. From now on there'll be two of us to shoulder things.

I'm also nervous, in case it goes wrong. Not the day – there are loads of people to fix problems at the vineyard, and Anita is being awesome about shielding me from stress. But I'm scared that the marriage will go wrong in one, three, maybe ten years' time – but then again, I'm sure it won't. How can it? It's weird. I'm in a daze, really. A can't-believe-it, this-is-all-a-dream daze.

I'll miss being engaged. That sounds so daft, but I will. Engagement is easy – it's all roses and flowers and diamonds. It's whirlwind excitement, and kissing, and laughter. Marriage doesn't have the same promise... I'm scared it'll be all broken washing machines and nagging and fry-ups. I so want to be a good wife. I want to look pretty every day,

be calm and in control, to cook apple pies and dumplings (without ever getting fat), and be supportive and lovely to J. I want to be the ultimate homemaker, and beautiful.

My main fear, of course, is that, after everything we have been through, J won't turn up tomorrow morning. Naturally. He's at home tonight, with his parents. We've spoken already today and his suit is ready, he's had a haircut and he's put petrol in the car. Tomorrow he's got to drive a fair way to the vineyard so – obviously – I'm worried sick that he'll crash before I can get to him. I'm scared his alarm clock won't go off. I'm scared it will, but then he'll decide not to come. I'm scared. .

I'm just scared. This is such a big step. It's really hitting me now. But I'll still go through with it. Oh – text message! It's from J. No! Is this it then? Do people call off weddings via text message these days? I had a friend who told her fiancé by e-mail – spineless I thought. It'd be very modern, though. Very 21st century.

Hang on, it says – "Can't wait for tomorrow. I love you more than anything and you'll be the best wife in the world. Too excited to sleep XXX. PS Don't be late!"

Aaaaah. ✳

Deadlines for this week

Pretty much everything should be in place now, with all the final arrangements coming together as you have planned. All that is left for you to do is apply yourself to the finishing touches, and make sure everyone else knows what they are doing.

☐ Try on your wedding gown and headpiece for the last time before the wedding and assemble it with the undergarments, shoes and jewellery.

☐ Confirm that the formalwear shop is delivering all the men's attire to the groom's home on the morning of the wedding.

☐ Touch base with your clergyman to be sure everything is in order for the marriage ceremony. Make copies of the special readings and give extras to the attendants.

☐ Tally up the guest response cards and add in the number of members of the wedding party to determine a final headcount.

☐ Confirm all the food and beverage details with the caterer, and provide the total number of attendees at the reception. Write the cheque for the balance due on the catering bill, to pay on the day of the wedding.

☐ Confirm all the decorating details with the florist, including delivery of flowers to the ceremony and reception venues. Arrange for the mothers' and grandmothers' flowers and fathers' and grandfathers' buttonholes to be delivered to where they will dress for the wedding. Make plans to pay the balance due on the florist's bill on the day of the wedding.

☐ Confirm the wedding cake delivery and set-up times with the baker. Remind the baker that you plan to freeze the top layer of your cake, and be sure that any family keepsakes used as decoration will be returned to you after the wedding. Write the cheque for the balance due on the baker's bill.

☐ Anticipate the toasts and/or speeches you and your new husband will want to offer at the reception, and finalise notes for them.

☐ Wrap the gifts for the members of the wedding party.

☐ Remind both sets of parents of who stands where in the formation of the receiving line at the reception.

☐ Put away any wedding gifts received in your new home so that you're ready to relax comfortably when you return from the honeymoon.

☐ Make up the bed in your new home with soft sheets and lots of pillows. Stock the refrigerator with wine and snacks for a romantic feast.

☐ Double-check the paperwork required by the clergyman.

☐ Start packing for the honeymoon.

One Week To Go

Last-minute jitters

Overwhelmed as the complexity of all the details and mounting stress hits a peak just before the Big Day? Even the most level-headed bride will have a panic attack or two juggling the last details into their proper places, so it's important to have a vehicle for relieving anxieties.

If you're not sleeping soundly and are snapping at those around you or have lost your appetite and sense of humour, it's time to back off and employ some mood-enhancement strategies. (In most cases, you just need a temporary escape to regain your balance, but don't hesitate to talk with your physician if you have more serious concerns.)

* First, take stock of the basics, like food and water. You're probably watching what you eat to be sure to fit into your wedding dress, but you need to be keeping plenty of food in your body and drinking enough water. Don't deprive yourself of a food craving, but try to keep it in moderation. Cut back on high-caffeine drinks and replace them with herbal tea or fruit juices.

* Try to get at least eight hours sleep per night, which is what you will need to feel rested. If your sleep quotient is off track, take advantage of the odd quiet moment and have a power nap.

* A massage or aromatherapy treatment might be a great cure for general body aches, while a manicure and pedicure offer the ultimate pamper. Although you'll be as busy as ever in the last weeks before the wedding, try to keep up with your exercise regimen or at least try to fit some walking and stretching in every day. Gentle yoga can help you maintain your physical flexibility and proper breathing techniques.

* Light some scented candles and fill the bath high for a bubble bath. Add a few drops of your favourite essential oils to help you relax. Dry off and don a thick dressing-gown before settling down for a soothing cup of peppermint or chamomile tea before bedtime.

* Make time to curl up with a good book or listen to your favourite music. Or take sole possession of the remote control and tune in to your favourite television show or movie.

* Stay connected with your friends and don't be shy about sharing your emotions with them as well as your fiancé. Employ some delegating strategies to people you can totally depend on to help lighten the load on your shoulders.

* Plan a night out at a comedy club to catch up on your daily dose of laughter or a casual dinner with your best mates.

" The day before my wedding I felt total calm. Everything was planned and everybody knew what they were doing. We had relatives staying over with friends nearby and there was such a great atmosphere – a real buzz of excitement. It all seemed so natural and it was just the best way to begin the celebrations. "

Beth, 29

One day to go

This is it. There is no turning back and all you can do now is enjoy yourself. Try to relax and accept that anything that hasn't been done by the end of the day won't be done and cannot be important.

Final countdown
Here is your last set of deadlines:

☐ Write a special thank-you note to both sets of parents from the two of you to express your appreciation for their love and support throughout your engagement. Arrange for it to be delivered with a floral arrangement to their home.

☐ Deliver the orders of service to a trusted family member or friend to pass out at the marriage ceremony.

☐ Write cheques with final payments for the organist, caterer, florist, baker and musicians.

☐ Prepare the clergyman's fee or make a contribution to your church or synagogue in his or her honour.

☐ Share the bridal spotlight with your attendants at a bridesmaids' luncheon. Present your attendants' gifts then or at the rehearsal, if you like.

☐ Join with all the members of the wedding party for supper after the rehearsal.

☐ Double-check with the ushers to be sure that they are clear on where family members and guests are to be seated.

☐ Invite the wedding party to sign a guest book at the rehearsal, if you like, so that they don't miss doing it with all the excitement on the Big Day.

☐ Enjoy the warmth of bringing your families together at the rehearsal, and offer a few toasts to special relatives and friends who have played big roles leading up to the wedding day, if you get the chance to have dinner together afterwards.

☐ Go to bed early for plenty of rest the night before the wedding.

The Big Day

Congratulations! You made it. You are going to be a bride. All the hard work that has gone into the planning over the last half-year or so will come to fruition today. This is the day of your dreams; it is your day, and you should enjoy every single minute of it.

The best advice for any bride is to try to sleep as late as possible into the day that you'll be married. Not only will you need the rest to fuel the energy you'll be burning throughout the day, but a good night's sleep will soften the under-eye circles that signal too many late nights. Even if you're not a big breakfast eater, give your stomach some nourishment right away and plan to graze until the time to start dressing for the wedding with a bunch of mini-meals.

Your wedding timetable

The final stages of preparation will be taking place throughout the day, and you will need to keep half an eye on those while allowing enough time for you to get ready yourself. All of the events centre around the ceremony. Below is a sample wedding day timetable to give you an idea of what should happen when so that you can keep things on track, assuming you are having an afternoon wedding.

9.00 a.m.

Lie in bed as long as you can before getting up and having a light breakfast.

Phone your fiancé to share your emotions and anticipation of the day. Unlike yours, his morning will be a leisurely one with his groomsmen, maybe including an early morning half-round of golf or a light brunch before he needs to get dressed for the pre-wedding photos later on.

9.30 a.m.

Shower and dress casually in a button-up shirt so as not to ruin your hair and make-up later.

While you are waiting for the hair and make-up stylists to arrive, glance over your packing list and tuck any last-minute items into your honeymoon suitcase.

10.30 a.m.

Your hair stylist should arrive and can start arranging your hair as discussed in your earlier sessions.

11.30 a.m.

Your bouquet and the corsages for the wedding party will arrive. The make-up artist should arrive around this time, along with the other women in the wedding party.

Enjoy the pampering as your make-up is applied. Sit back while the nail technician adds a protective topcoat to your manicure and pedicure.

12.30 p.m.

You should make time for a quick break for lunch before getting into your wedding outfit.

The photographer should arrive shortly, if he or she has not been with you all morning, and will begin to take photos of you and the female wedding party getting ready and in formal groups.

At around this time the flowers will be arranged at the church and reception sites, the caterer will be overseeing both the meal preparation and the setting of the reception tables, and the baker will be adding finishing touches to the decoration of the wedding cake.

1.00 p.m.

The photographer will leave and make his or her way to the groom's house to take pictures of him and his ushers as they leave for the ceremony site.

At the same time, the florist should arrive with the buttonholes.

1.30 p.m.

The limousines will arrive at both the bride's and groom's homes.

1.45 p.m.

The mother of the bride and bridesmaids leave the bride's house.The groom and his party leave the groom's house.

2.00 p.m.

The groom and best man take their places inside, and remain seated at the front.

The ushers will greet the guests who will have begun arriving at the church, and escort them to their seats to enjoy the medley of prelude tunes.

2.15 p.m.

The bride and her father depart the family or bride's house.

On arrival at the ceremony site, the wedding director will help the group to settle and the photographer will take photographs of you and your bridesmaids before the start of the ceremony.

The clergyman will come to each group to check everything is in order and offer a short prayer and blessing.

You'll get ready to take your place at the entrance to the chapel.

2.30 p.m.

The church bells peal and/or the processional music begins. You take your father's arm to step slowly up the aisle and begin the ceremony.

At around this time the baker will be delivering the cake and setting up at the reception site, as will the musicians.

3.30 p.m.

You and your groom are pronounced husband and wife, you kiss, and start the recessional. You pose for pictures before you all leave for the reception site – the wedding party departing first.

4.00 p.m.

Everyone should now be at the reception site. While the guests are already enjoying a cocktail and refreshment, the two of you will quickly take your places in the receiving line, if you are having one, signalling the guests to offer their personal congratulations. Alternatively, the MC will announce the bridal party and you enter.

6.30 p.m.

The meal is served and then a glass of champagne is given to each guest, signalling the best man to stand and start the toasts and speechmaking.

8.00 p.m.

The two of you cut the cake and dessert will be served to the guests as you circulate among the tables to greet guests.

9.30 p.m.

The two of you will dance the bridal waltz, and thank each of your parents before you throw your bouquet and you and your husband make a dash for the getaway car and the first totally private moment to celebrate the day.

Survival tactics

A wedding day is like no other day of your life. For this one day you are going to be the centre of attention and will probably be feeling charged with energy and emotion. Most brides say their wedding day goes by in a flash, but it is a long day and you should be prepared for it.

* An empty stomach, or one filled with the wrong types of food, can play havoc with your nerves. Avoid anything very fatty or high in sugar and pass on the carbonated drinks. Instead get plenty of water inside you and have a light meal before leaving for the ceremony.

* It goes without saying that you should take it easy the night before the Big Day. Too much alcohol will leave you feeling groggy and smoking before you go to bed may well disrupt your sleep, as nicotine is a stimulant. Limit your caffeine intake on the morning of the preparations, and if the champagne is flowing, go easy on it, or avoid it altogether until you get to the wedding reception.

* Make sure you leave enough time to pamper yourself. Take a long bath first thing and have the hair stylist and make-up artist arrive with plenty of time to work in a relaxed manner. You don't want to leave for the ceremony feeling stressed out.

* If you have a blemish on the day (and it can happen) whatever you do, do not make it worse. Use a medicated ointment to dry it out (toothpaste and vodka have been known to work too) and have your make-up artist deal with it for you.

* Try to steal quiet moments to yourself as you prepare, even if this means locking yourself in the bathroom for five minutes of deep breathing.

* Repeat a mantra as a quick and effective form of mind control. If you know you are going to get jittery as you walk up the aisle, think of something you can be saying in time with your steps.

One Week To Go

Index

A

accessories 72, 74–5, 81, 100
  bridesmaids' 69
  wedding 114
announcement, engagement
  16, 100

B

bank account, joint 125
banns 43
beautician 76
beauty programme 76
best man 57, 90, 94
  responsibilities of 28, 58, 88,
    90–1, 92, 139
birthstones 15
bouquet(s): bride's 48, 52
  bridesmaids' 26
  to preserve 114
  "toss" 59, 114
bridal registry 61, 101, 109,
  119
bridal shower 116
bride: bouquet 48, 52
  gown 66–7, 70–1, 72–3, 80,
    81
bride's father, responsibilities
  of 28, 107, 139
bride's mother 139
  responsibilities of 28, 57
bride's parents, responsibilities
  of 16, 50
bridesmaids: accessories 69
  bouquets 26
  at ceremony 126
  dresses 26, 67, 69, 100, 127
  gifts for 69
  looking after 29, 118, 124
  luncheon 29, 137
  see also chief bridesmaid
budget 24, 30, 31, 32, 39, 43
  for gown 72, 73
  for honeymoon 87
  for reception 50, 53, 62
  buttonholes 48, 52, 86,134,
    139

C

cake: 55, 101, 114, 119, 134,
  138
  cutting 139
  groom's 114
  top layer 55, 134
caterers 55, 63, 100, 124,
  134, 138,
celebrant 38, 39–40, 41, 109
  see also clergyman
ceremony 39–41, 139
  civil 41, 42
  interfaith 38
  Jewish 52
  music at 42, 100, 139
  outdoor 43, 44
  planning 100
  religious 38, 39–40, 42
  seating at 107, 137, 139
  traditional 38
  venue 38, 39, 41, 44, 45
checklist: one-day 137
  one-month 124–5
  one-week 134
  three-month 100–1
  two-month 114
chief bridesmaid 28, 57, 69,
  75, 126
children at wedding 28, 114,
  126
chuppah 52
clergyman 38, 39–40, 134,
  139
  to pay 39, 91, 137
colour scheme 26, 52
compromise, importance of 18,
  23, 24, 38
confetti, alternatives to 60
corsages 26, 52
counselling, premarital 40,
  100, 104–5, 109

D

dances at reception 58–9,
  107, 139

date, to choose 24
decoration: floral 26, 52
  table 26, 48, 52
  themed 26
  unusual 52
delegating tasks 108, 136
dessert 55
destination wedding 41, 43,
  44
  web sites 33, 45, 95
diamonds 15, 19
diet, healthy 78, 79, 108, 136,
  140
divorced parents: 16
  inviting 103
  at wedding 44, 106–7
drinks 26, 49, 55

E

engagement: to announce 16
  party 17
  see also ring(s)
exercise 78–9, 108, 136

F

family tensions 106–7
  see also divorced parents;
    step-relatives
favours 63
florist 48, 52, 101, 134
flower girl 28
flowers: at ceremony 52
  delivery 134, 138
  to order 101
  at reception 26, 48, 52,
food see menu
formalwear, men's 26, 86, 90,
  100, 127, 134
  styles 93, 94

G

gemstones 15
gift list 102, 109, 119
  see also bridal registry
gifts: alternative 61
  for attendants 117, 137

for bridesmaids 69, 117
engagement 17
for groom 124
wedding 61, 101, 134
for wedding party 114
see also bridal registry; bridal
    shower
going-away outfit 114
groom 139
  responsibilities of 86–7, 94
  transportation 51
groom's parents,
  responsibilities of 16, 17
guest book/register 57, 114,
  137
guests 26, 101, 106
  accommodation for 36, 101
  numbers 32, 44, 134
  transportation 51
  see also wedding party

H
hair 76, 81, 114, 138
handbag 75
headpiece 74, 75
hen night 92, 112–13, 116,
  118
honeymoon: arrangements for
  84–5, 86, 01, 124
  destination 87
  getaway 51, 59, 86, 91, 139
  travel tips 88–9
  web sites 95

I
in-laws 38, 106
inoculations 43, 88, 101, 114
insurance 15, 129
Internet: announcing
  engagement on 16
  information on 31, 55, 62, 66,
    84, 87
  see also web sites
invitations 102–3, 114
  to engagement party 17
  inserts 102
  themed 26, 102
  wording 103, 107

J
jewellery 19, 74
  bridesmaids' 69
  see also ring(s); wedding
    band(s)

K
keeping fit 78–9

L
last-minute checks 127
legal requirements 43, 101
  for destination weddings 43,
    44, 101
  for surname 115, 125
  for venues 41, 44
lingerie 74

M
magazines 22, 30, 56, 66, 74,
  80
make-up 76–7, 81, 124, 138
manicure 29, 76, 77, 80, 124
marriage certificate 43, 89
  overseas 43
matron-of-honour 28
medical checkup 79
menu 48–9, 54–5, 100
  special requirements 55
music: at ceremony 42, 100,
  119, 139
  at reception 26, 49, 53, 100,
    101, 109, 124
  for video 56, 101

N
"new home" cards 101, 102

O
officiant see celebrant
overseas wedding see
  destination wedding

P
page boy 28
pampering 124, 136, 140
parents: dance 59
  to thank 137
  see also bride's parents;
    groom's parents

parking spaces 114
party: engagement 17
  hen 92, 112–13, 116
  see also stag night
passport, to obtain 43
pedicure 29, 76, 77, 80, 124
photography 56, 63, 101, 107,
  109, 124
  pre-wedding 138–9
place cards 58, 102
place settings 26, 52
planning: deadlines 108, 134,
  137
  financial 31, 32
  honeymoon 88–9, 95
  initial 24
  premarital counselling 40, 100,
    104–5
  resources 109
pre-wedding nerves 98–9,
  132–3, 136
problems: within marriage 105
  on wedding day 127, 128
professionals, using 24, 30,
  62, 63, 127
programme, wedding 60, 114
proposal 6–7, 18

R
readings 42, 100, 122, 134
receiving line 57, 107, 134,
  139
reception: conventions 57–9
  dances at 58–9, 107, 139
  drinks 26, 49, 55
  flowers 26, 48, 52
  menu 48–9, 54–5, 100
  music 26, 49, 53, 100, 101,
    124
  running order 49, 139
  seating at 29, 58, 106
  style 48, 50
  time of 54
  venue 45, 50
registry office 41, 43, 45
rehearsal, wedding 29, 86, 90,
  101, 114, 117, 122, 126, 137
  dinner 91, 114, 123, 126, 137
relaxation 136, 140
residency requirements 41, 44

response cards 102
ring(s): antique 14, 19
  to choose 12, 14–15
  exchanging 38
  own design 14
  to reject 18
  resources 19
  see also wedding band(s)

S

seating: at ceremony 107, 137, 139
  at reception 29, 58, 106
second marriages 17, 40, 93, 105
shoes 74–5, 81
  bridesmaids' 69
shower, bridal 116
showstoppers 33, 60, 119
sleep, importance of 79, 108, 136, 138, 140
speeches 49, 58, 91, 94, 134, 139
stag night 90, 92, 94, 112
stationery 101, 102–3
  resources 19, 109
  see also invitations; thank-you notes
step-relatives 44, 106, 107
surname: options 115

T

table decorations 26, 48, 52
tanning, fake 77
thank-you notes 17, 101, 102, 114, 118, 124
theme, wedding 22–3, 24–5, 52, 55, 102
  to coordinate 26
  resources 33
  seasonal 25, 26
timetable for wedding day 138–9
toasts 17, 58, 91, 134, 139
train of gown 72
transportation 51, 86, 91, 101 129, 139
travel tips 88–9

U

umbrella 75, 124
unity candle 42, 60
ushers 137, 139
  at ceremony 126
  formalwear for 26, 90, 93
  responsibilities of 28, 60

V

veil 74
venue: to choose 36–7, 41
  contract with 41, 44, 100
  legal requirements for 41, 44
  for reception 50
  for wedding night 84, 86
videography 56, 101, 124
visa, to obtain 43
vows: exchanging 38, 42, 122
  personalised 42, 100

W

water intake 79, 108, 136, 140
weather, protection from 75, 124
websites: accessories 81
  caterers 63
  ceremony sites 45
  changing your name 119
  confetti 129
  contingency plans 129
  dance lessons 129
  destination weddings 33
  dresses 81
  favours 63
  flowers 63
  gift list 119
  hen parties 119
  honeymoon 95
  insurance 129
  menswear 95
  music 63
  premarital counselling 109
  photography 63
  registration 45
  religion 109
  rings 19
  showstoppers 33
  speeches 95

stationery 109
themed weddings 33
transportation 129
wedding: accessories 114
  children at 28, 114, 126
  cost 14, 24, 30, 31, 32; see also budget
  divorced parents at 44, 106–7
  gifts 61, 101, 134
  oversees see destination wedding
  planning 24, 63, 108, 109, 134, 137
  programme 60, 114
  themed 22–3, 24–5, 26, 33
  timetable 138–9
  timing of 24, 32, 39
  venue 36–7, 41, 50
wedding band(s) 15, 114
wedding cake 55, 101, 114, 134, 138
  cutting 139
  top layer 55, 134
wedding consultant 24, 30, 33, 43
wedding coordinator 41, 44
wedding gown: to choose 66, 68, 72–3, 80
  fittings 72, 100
  to preserve 73
  resources 81
  second-hand 66–7, 73, 81
  to store 73
  styles 70–1
  themed 68
wedding night, venue for 84, 86
wedding party 28, 40, 126, 137, 138, 139
  seating at reception 58
wedding planner see wedding consultant
wedding rehearsal 29, 90, 101, 114, 117, 122, 126, 127
weight, to lose 78, 79, 80
weight training 79